MW01280275

Text Messages to my Children

Essays on Life & Faith from a Father's Heart – Volume 1

Mark Martin-Williams

Copyright © 2023 Mark Martin-Williams
All rights reserved.
ISBN 979-8-218-15101-0

To Misha, Keira and Saskia:
With all of my gratitude and affection.

Introduction

Text Messages to My Children was borne out of my desire to communicate with my kids about life and faith before they left home. We had, of course, had many discussions along the way, but I felt I hadn't been able to share my heart as fully and clearly as I would have liked.

As I considered what I might do, I landed on the idea of sending my kids text messages. This would give me the opportunity to share what was on my mind, while also being able to carefully consider what I was trying to say. It would give me the opportunity to distill ideas down so my kids could take 5-10 minutes to read them when they had breaks in their busy schedules.

Initially, I started sending short devotional texts with just a few sentences and a Bible verse. But I struggled with this, because I don't approach my faith quite this way. I still felt text messages were the right medium, but I needed to use my own voice. I wanted to share with them what I was thinking as if they were adults, because they very nearly were.

So, I decided my best offering would be to share with my children the story of my own faith; to share where it came from, and where I hoped it was going. I especially wanted to share with them where it was in the present, as it related to particular verses or passages I was studying in my Bible that very day.

I do not have the ability to understand exactly what my kids might need to hear in the places where they are, but if I have the courage, and am willing to be appropriately vulnerable, I can share with them what I am experiencing and thinking about where I am today, or maybe where I was at other times in my life. And maybe this might help them learn how to think more spiritually, to find a better vantage point from which to observe their own lives.

I realize sometimes these thoughts might not mean much to my kids where they are on a given day. But sometimes these thoughts might connect with them exactly where they are. So, initially, my plan was to collect these essays in a three-ring binder I could give to my kids, to revisit later on in their lives, if they wished.

However, over the first couple of years of writing these texts, something happened that I did not expect – I truly began to find my voice. I began to learn how to speak in a particular way that felt uniquely personal to me. So, I went back and edited my earlier texts to fit better with the voice I had begun to discover. Rather than a three-ring binder, I thought it might be more meaningful if I could offer my children a book instead, which brings me to the present day.

If my family members are the only people who see these essays, I will be content. But as I have shared them with a couple of other close friends, they have encouraged me to make them available to other people. If that is you, and this book has found its way into your hands, my wish is that it will be encouraging to you.

My greatest hope is you might be able to see some of your own story; that it might help you to feel less alone; that we might become travelling companions of sorts along this spiritual journey.

One final note – Because this book is a collection of essays, it does not necessarily need to be read in order. Some of the essays build on the previous ones, but each essay could be read independently and make sense. Lastly, I imagine, on some of the longer essays, you might doubt that anyone would send such long text messages… But I assure you, every single essay was originally sent as a text message!

1
The First Text – High-Sounding Nonsense

Good morning kids! I was thinking last night I have failed part of my role as your father. I have not encouraged you all in your journeys towards God as deliberately as I should have. Moreover, I have rarely shared either the experiences of my own journey, or the things I am working through here and now.

Because we are all busy, I was thinking I will start to send you texts many mornings with a verse I am thinking about and how it relates to situations in life and in faith. Sometimes it might not be helpful to you, but it is my greatest privilege to be in relationships with all of you, and I don't want to miss the opportunity to encourage you all to know and seek God while you are still at home with me for a little longer.

The verse I'm thinking about today is Colossians 2:8 from the New Living Translation:

"Don't let anyone capture you with empty philosophies and high-sounding nonsense that come from human thinking and from the spiritual powers of this world, rather than from Christ."

We are flooded with all kinds of messages about what is right and wrong, and true and false. We are influenced through social media, the news, and even through our friendships. It is easy to follow along with many of these ideas because they often seem to make sense.

This is because God has created a moral universe we can all see. All people acknowledge there is right and wrong, and they even assume most people define those things the same way.

The problem is, for a moral universe to be consistent it has to be based on something absolutely true. If people don't believe in an ultimate truth, they will base their truth on themselves and what they think in their own minds.

These personal philosophies often sound sophisticated in their claims they don't need faith in an invisible God. The great irony, though, is they are making an even bolder statement of faith. They unknowingly are suggesting ultimate truth comes from themselves, even though they know they are not worthy.

Unfortunately, these personal philosophies do not all agree with one another because each one has placed a different human god at the center of it. And the inevitable resolution to this conundrum is to feebly acknowledge I am the god of my world and you are the god of your world, so whatever I believe is true for me and whatever you believe is true for you.

In the end, the philosophies that come from human thinking are really just opinions that don't have any reliable basis to claim a Truth that is ultimate for all people. I believe this is because our lives are meant to be captured by Christ, not by empty philosophies based only on human thinking.

2
Why I Believe There is a God

Good morning kids! I have a couple of verses today. This is a bit longer, but it is important to me to let you know I take you all seriously. You are all intelligent people who are capable of thinking deeply. God has given us brains to think through our faith so it will have a firm foundation.

Nehemiah 9:6:
"You alone are the LORD; You have made heaven, the heaven of heavens, with all their host, the earth and everything on it, the seas and all that is in them, and You preserve them all."

Romans 1:20:
"For ever since the world was created, people have seen the earth and sky. Through everything God made, they can clearly see his invisible qualities—his eternal power and divine nature. So they have no excuse for not knowing God."

When it comes to what we believe, it is easy to just say we believe there is a God and He created everything because that is what the majority of people seem to believe. But I want you all to really use your minds to understand why you believe in God.

As you get older you will come across many people who don't share this view. Many of the most educated people, especially, will be loudly against the possibility of there being a God. These people will say they believe in science, not God. This sounds kind of sophisticated and modern, but really it is just as much a statement of faith as the person who says they believe in God.

Paul would go on to say in the next verse, Romans 1:21, "For although they knew God, they neither glorified Him as God nor gave thanks to Him, but their thinking became futile and their foolish hearts were darkened."

I believe God created science. I believe when He created everything, He used, and continues to use science to bring about His will and His plan for our world. This doesn't mean He can't do things without using science. He is all powerful and can do whatever He wants, but He has created an amazing universe that can be understood better by science. Scientific understanding allows us to observe our world with greater and deeper wonder.

Remember, there are really only two possible ideas for where the world and people came from. Forget about the arguments over evolution, or whether God created the world in seven 24-hour days. There are really only two views for creation: either God created the heavens and the earth and everything in it, or He didn't.

If He didn't create it, this means matter (the physical stuff the earth is made of) is eternal. The people who believe in science, but not God, have to believe the universe, and matter itself, are eternal, that they have existed forever with no beginning.

Furthermore, they have to believe matter organized itself randomly and blew itself up, eventually resulting in the universe, and then somehow further organized itself by total chance into the heavens and the earth and everything in it, (including people with sight, taste, touch, smell and conscious minds).

For people who don't believe in God, this is a statement of faith, because this cannot be proven in a laboratory. No scientist has been able to make something come from nothing. It is their religion, and they accept it completely on faith.

For me, I think it is more likely there is a God who created the universe and everything in it. It seems more reasonable to me that the Spirit of God is eternal rather than physical matter; that He has no beginning and no end; that He has infinite power; that He has the power to create matter and science and the heavens and the earth and everything in it.

Don't be intimidated by the arguments surrounding God and the creation of the earth. You are intelligent and I believe God wants you to know Him with all of your minds.

<u>3</u>
Why I Think We Are Here

Good morning kids! Today's verses are from Psalm 139:13-18.

"For you created my inmost being;
you knit me together in my mother's womb.
I praise you because I am fearfully and wonderfully made;
your works are wonderful,
I know that full well.
My frame was not hidden from you
when I was made in the secret place,
when I was woven together in the depths of the earth.
Your eyes saw my unformed body;
all the days ordained for me were written in your book
before one of them came to be.
How precious to me are your thoughts, O God!
How vast is the sum of them!
Were I to count them,
they would outnumber the grains of sand—
when I awake, I am still with you."

In my previous text, I talked about why I believe in God and why I think it is the most reasonable explanation of creation. Today, I want to look at why WE are here.

Some people believe there is a God, but they don't believe He is personal. These people are generally called "Deists." They believe God was the "first mover." He is like a watch maker who created the world and set it in motion and then stepped back. They don't believe He has been personally involved in history since creation. These people don't believe in miracles, nor do they believe Jesus was God's son.

This philosophy became especially popular in the late 1600's, during the "Enlightenment," or "The Age of Reason." Coincidentally, this period lined up exactly with the formation of the United States. The majority of the founding fathers of the United States were Deists. These people thought the human mind holds ultimate truth apart from God. This is the main way the world thinks today: when we're enlightened by the truth of our own minds, the world will improve. They think the truth is from us, not from God.

Our verses from the Psalms indicate, however, that God is very involved in the world and in making us. Throughout the Bible we are told things like Isaiah 48:17, "I am the LORD your God, who teaches you what is best for you, who directs you in the way you should go." He knows us and was very specific about who He made us to be.

When we seek to know Him, He will show us more and more of what is true, and because it is based in Him and His power, it will reveal the real source of truth that is beyond human minds and politics and governments.

God wants us to glorify Him, but not because He is conceited. He wants us to glorify and worship Him because we were created to worship, and if we don't worship Him, we will worship our own selves and our ideas and other created things, just like the people in the Old Testament who worshiped golden calves.

We like to think we are more sophisticated today. But really, we have just made different idols. The only difference is we have made them out of ideas and beliefs from our minds, instead of things made from gold.

When we learn to let go of trying to be responsible for determining the meaning of life from our own minds, and learn to seek the actual Source of life that is in God and from God, we will discover our real selves. It will be full of freedom and joy, because it will be based on the eternal faithfulness of God.

4
Why I Think Belief in Jesus is Reliable

Good morning kids! Today's text is a little bit longer, but hopefully you will have a few minutes of downtime to read it sometime today. The last two days I've talked about why I believe in God, and then why I believe God created us to have a personal relationship with Him. Now I want to explain why I believe in Jesus from an intellectual perspective. Today's verses are 1 Corinthians 15:3-8:

"For what I received I passed on to you as of first importance: that Christ died for our sins according to the Scriptures, that he was buried, that he was raised on the third day according to the Scriptures, and that he appeared to Cephas, and then to the Twelve. After that, he appeared to more than five hundred of the brothers and sisters at the same time, most of whom are still living, though some have fallen asleep. Then he appeared to James, then to all the apostles, and last of all he appeared to me also."

This passage is important because it shows Christianity, and the life, death and resurrection of Jesus are based in history. Paul spent 1 1/2 years in the town of Corinth from AD 51-52. We know this because of the agreement between the history recorded in the book of Acts by Luke with the history contained in Paul's own letters.

Paul wrote the book of 1 Corinthians a few years later in AD 55 because he was concerned with rumors he was hearing about the church he had set up in Corinth. When we read this today, it's easy to forget Paul and the other apostles were trying to create churches for a new belief system based on Jesus. There were no such things as these sorts of churches before they came along. There were only synagogues and also altars to pagan gods.

Also, they had only recently, at about the time Paul was writing this letter, begun to be called "Christians" in a few of the larger towns. Mostly, they were viewed as a random group that had distorted the Jewish faith.

One other complication was that this belief was one of the first to deliberately cross national boundaries. Some of the apostles were establishing churches in Jewish towns, while Paul and some other apostles were establishing churches in non-Jewish towns outside of Israel. This made it especially important to determine what their beliefs were, so it made sense to all the new churches regardless of where they were located.

We know from Acts and Paul's letters that the apostles had meetings to try to determine what they did and did not believe. In the passage above, Paul reminds the church at Corinth that the core belief of the new Christian churches being established, whether in Jewish towns or non-Jewish (gentile) towns, was that Jesus lived, then died for our sins, was buried, and then raised on the third day, all according to the Jewish scriptures.

Remember, what we call the "Old Testament" today was the only Bible these early Christians had, and they relied on it to seek God AND to know Jesus.

Paul goes on to remind them this is not something they had to believe on blind faith. He tells them Jesus appeared to Peter, who would've been familiar to them. And then He appeared to the 12 disciples. And then he mentions another time He appeared to 500 believers at the same time. And then he appeared to James and then later to Paul on the road to Damascus.

It is generally believed Jesus appeared to James, who was one of Jesus's brothers, because James did not yet believe his brother could really be the Son of God. After appearing to James, James went on to become the head of the churches being established in Jerusalem. I imagine it would've taken very convincing proof of Jesus's resurrection to convince James his own earthly brother was the Living Son of God so that James changed the course of his life to establish a very unpopular church; a church that was opposed by both the Jews in Jerusalem and by the Romans that ruled the government.

James, like nearly all of the other apostles, would go onto a martyr's death. Why would all of these people who knew Jesus before and after the crucifixion choose such difficult lives of proclaiming the truth of Jesus, knowing it would lead to painful deaths, unless they were positive they had seen and touched the risen Jesus?

Also, why would they do this unless the life they found in the Living Christ gave them joy and peace in spite of their difficult lives?

Paul goes on to say many of these people who had seen the resurrected Jesus are still living, although some had died. His point was, if the Corinthians didn't accept Paul's word, they could verify it by seeking out the word of one of the many other eyewitnesses to the resurrection of Jesus who were still living at that time.

I know these last few texts have been a little lengthy, but it is important to me you kids know why I think you can trust in God and believe in Jesus. These last few texts, I hope, gave you a fairly brief summary of a faith that is not blind, but that has a thoughtful foundation in rational critical thinking. I don't expect you to just believe whatever I do, but I do want you to know a bit about why I believe what I do, and I hope it gives you some thoughts that might help you along the way on your own journeys.

5
Why Did Jesus Have to Die?

Good morning kids! Today's verse is Colossians 2:2-3:

"I want you to have complete confidence that you understand God's mysterious plan, which is Christ Himself. In Him lie hidden all the treasures of wisdom and knowledge."

While belief in Jesus is the fundamental Christian belief, I don't think it's necessarily easy. As Paul says, it is part of a mysterious plan. It's a hidden treasure. It's frustrating to me how simple many Christians make it seem.

I do think there are some people who are blessed to have a natural faith, but I have always been the kind of person that has to wrestle with ideas for a long time before I can trust them. Personally, to this day, I continue to sometimes wonder: "Why did we need Jesus to come?"

We know God created people with free will, so they could choose to follow Him and believe in Him or not. He also gave everyone the ability to mostly know the difference between right and wrong. God created that and put it in the minds and hearts of all people.

He then chose a particular nation, the Jews in the Old Testament, to give even more specific instructions to. He gave them the written law. He showed them specifically what they needed to do to follow Him. But as we see in the Old

Testament, people could not perfectly follow the law, or even live in perfect accordance with an innate sense of morality.

And this is the point where I often get stuck. I wonder why God couldn't just forgive everyone and move on. It was evident that people could not perfectly follow God, so why was it necessary to send Jesus? Why couldn't God just forgive us without Jesus?

I think it was because we wouldn't have been able to understand or appreciate His forgiveness. We would not have realized the significance of His grace and mercy. We needed to witness a human person born of flesh and blood who could actually live a human life and carry out the law perfectly. He had to be human. We could not accept it any other way.

And to take this a step further, Jesus had to be inexplicably *punished* for carrying out the law perfectly for us. If *He* was not punished, *we* would have had to continue to bear the punishment; to bear the ultimate consequences of our sin. Due to the fact that God created a perfectly moral universe, an innocent person had to bear the consequences of sin instead. This was the only way people who deserved the punishment could go free.

By dying as a human and rising again, He established an historical event where He stepped in to interrupt the cycle of fallenness that we see throughout the Old Testament. He was able to offer us His perfection; offer us His Spirit; so we could share in His perfection by faith alone, rather than by following laws.

Before His sacrifice, there was nothing we could do to make ourselves perfect; to make ourselves worthy to stand before God. But after His sacrifice, we became able to share in Christ's perfection, so we also became allowed to stand with Him before God without guilt, even though we don't deserve it.

Christ's Spirit is in us, and it makes us worthy. It makes us the people God created us to be. It is Christ in us that praises God outside of us. It is the heart of God's mysterious plan.

6
Behold, I Stand at the Door and Knock

Good morning kids! Today's verse is Revelation 3:20:

"Behold, I stand at the door and knock; if anyone hears My voice and opens the door, I will come in and eat with that person, and they with Me."

I suspect this is a well-known verse to you. We are likely to hear speakers quote this verse, often in reference to how Jesus is knocking on a non-Christian's heart. While it is true Jesus wants everyone to know Him, I don't think this was the intention of Jesus' message here.

Jesus actually spoke those words to a Christian church in a town called Laodicea. Before He spoke this verse, He was judging them for being lukewarm. They weren't hot or cold in their relationship with God. They were mostly interested in being comfortable and didn't want to do the hard work of really seeking God and following the example of Jesus.

Jesus was telling the Christians in this church they were the ones who needed to recognize their shortcomings, to be serious about committing themselves to a relationship with Jesus. He was calling them into the kind of relationship where He comes in and dines with them.

And He is outside the doors of our hearts and minds too. He wants us to invite Him in; to come in and have a relationship with us. This happens over and over, I think. Each new day we can invite Him in or not.

Some days I leave Him outside and ignore the knocking, because I'm tired or angry or depressed. I decide I'd rather be consumed by my own self-pity and busyness.

Some days I'm totally oblivious to His being outside the door, because things are going well and I don't feel like I really need Him that day.

Some days I pile furniture up against the door and I don't want Him to come in, because I'm afraid of what He might tell me. I feel like He would be ashamed of me if He saw what was happening on my side of the door.

And some days I let Him in. Those are always the best days.

I think it's odd I know my best life is the one I live with Jesus, and yet I often fight against it as if I don't really need Him or want Him. Fortunately, God is faithful. If we are willing to turn down the volume in our souls a bit, we will find He is there knocking each new morning.

7
Knowing God in the Present Tense

Good morning kids! It says in Psalm 27:13, "I remain confident of this: I will see the goodness of the LORD in the land of the living."

I am bothered by how Christians tend to talk about their faith with a heavy emphasis on going to heaven. I believe in heaven, but I don't think it should be the focus of our faith.

When we share our faith with one another, and especially when we share our faith with people who believe differently than us, we shouldn't be focusing on going to heaven, because the goodness of God is evident in the land of living. We are meant to experience His goodness in our lives today. He is not withholding His goodness until we die.

The focus on heaven turns faith in God almost into a bargain, as if we're saying, "Okay, I'll believe in you as long as I get to go to heaven." It's the "what's in it for me" sort of faith. It is not about relationship.

God intends us to know Him and to experience His goodness in the land of the living, through a relationship with Him, in the day-to-day living of our lives, here and now. Knowing God and walking with Jesus day-to-day is how we were meant to live, because it allows us to see His goodness in the present tense.

8
Spacious Places

Good morning kids! It says in Psalm 18:19:

"He brought me out into a spacious place; he rescued me because he delighted in me."

I love this imagery of God bringing us into spacious places. David used this phrase about spacious places a few times in his Psalms. At the time he wrote this particular one, David was being pursued by Saul, and we know from the historical books of the Bible that he was often hiding in small caves in the desert during these times.

We have a tendency to hide in small, tight places in our minds and spirits. Sometimes we feel like we'll be trapped in those places forever. It can be so dark, and yet we are often unwilling to leave, because we're afraid we'll just get more lost.

And those places are lonely. We feel like no one will be able to find us. And, perhaps even more discouraging, we are certain they would not be able to understand or appreciate what we are going through even if they could find us.

But regardless of what is happening in our lives, when we are in those small and dark places, remember that God loves us, and He has already rescued us. Jesus Himself descended into the darkest possible place to rescue us. And He will continue to rescue us again and again as we learn to trust Him.

Even when we feel cramped or trapped, God will bring us into spacious places in our spirits where He will take care of us regardless of our circumstances. This is how we learn to trust in His goodness and love for us. The experience of being delivered from dark and cramped places into the bright and open places of the Spirit makes us strong, so we become people who can endure hard times with hope and peace and joy.

9
Be Joyful Always

Good morning kids! It says in 1 Thessalonians 5:16-18:

"Always be joyful. Never stop praying. Be thankful in all circumstances, for this is God's will for you who belong to Christ Jesus."

These verses are often quoted around Thanksgiving, admonishing us to be thankful as we sit around a large feast, enjoying the benefits of living in a time of considerable peace and prosperity, at least in our corner of the world.

We don't recognize how unusual this admonishment actually is. Paul was writing this to the church in Thessalonica, encouraging them because they were facing significant persecution from their community that did not like this new Christian church that had been established in their town.

So, it is in the face of suffering that Paul says to be joyful always, pray continually, and give thanks regardless of circumstances. How much more does it apply to people like us who are very comfortable by comparison?

I think it is also significant Paul says this is God's will for us. People are always wondering what God's will is for them, like it is a total mystery. While some of it is indeed mysterious, these are some parts of God's will for us that are not.

Be joyful always. This is real joy, and it is based on the love of God shown to us in Jesus. It cannot be taken away and it is not dependent on any outside circumstances in our lives.

When we allow this joy into our hearts and minds, we will automatically start to pray continually, but not with mechanical kinds of prayers. We will pray and talk to God as we go about our days because we will realize He is present in our lives, and we will want to relate to Him as if in a conversation.

And then we will give thanks in all circumstances because we will become aware of the tremendous gift we have been given—the gift of relating to God through Jesus, because His Spirit is within us at all times, regardless of the things happening outside of us.

<u>10</u>
Every Good Thing

Good morning kids! It says in Psalm 34:10:

"Young lions lack and go hungry, but those who seek the LORD will never lack any good thing."

In the wilderness, young lions are a symbol of strength. Of all the creatures, they are the most able to go out and get what they need to survive by their own power. These young lions are like people who seek to meet their needs and find their happiness in the world by their own efforts.

They think the things they obtain will feed them and satisfy them, but the next day they will wake up hungry again. This is the way of the world, and it is a trap I have fallen into most of my life.

But we are told those who seek the Lord will lack no good thing. This is another Psalm David wrote from the desert when he was in hiding. He did not have any physical comforts, but he was saying, even in those conditions, he would lack no good things if he sought the Lord.

So then, the really good things must not have been palaces and clothes and feasts. What we forget is the Lord is always seeking us and He is not far away. When we don't find Him, it is either because we're not seeking Him at all, or because we're not looking very hard.

Often, we are looking for Him in places where we should know He is not going to be. We hope God will make us comfortable with physical, tangible gifts that money can buy without requiring our hearts.

But every truly good thing is in the Lord, and those are the things He wants to give each of us in abundance. When we truly seek the Lord Himself, when our hope is in finding Him rather than in finding personal peace and prosperity, He promises to give us every good thing.

Keep in mind, "every good thing" is much better than what our weak imaginations can comprehend. The peace and the joy and the contentment that every person craves is in the Lord, we just need to train our hearts to seek these good things in Him instead of in things that were never meant to provide true joy.

11
Peace That Passes Understanding

Good morning kids! Today's verses are Philippians 4:6-7:

"Don't worry about anything; instead, pray about everything. Tell God what you need, and thank him for all he has done. Then you will experience God's peace, which exceeds anything we can understand. His peace will guard your hearts and minds as you live in Christ Jesus."

This peace that surpasses understanding is something I want more and more the older I get. I struggle with worry. And I have spent a shameful amount of energy trying to find relief from worrying by seeking things other than God.

Oftentimes, I have sought good things in my efforts to escape anxiety and find peace, like trying to enjoy you kids as much as I can. But while our relationships are a tremendous gift and blessing, they are a gift FROM God; they are not God Himself.

Sometimes I try to hide from worrying, thinking it will just go away if I ignore it. I preoccupy myself with hobbies or projects. This, just like procrastinating on homework, makes it far worse. The anxiety piles up and becomes overwhelming.

Paul says the way to find peace that passes beyond understanding is to pray about everything; to lay all of our concerns before God. We are also told to do this with a thankful attitude. I think this is because, even in the midst of our anxiety, we can recall He has already given us so much that is good.

This seems easy enough, but I struggle with prayer. I often feel as if I don't understand the way to do it correctly. Fortunately, I think this prayer we are called into is something we are intended to do all day, kind of like breathing.

It is an attitude where we talk to God throughout our day, about the things that are happening one by one as they come in the course of life. As we learn to live this way, we will get true peace that passes understanding which will guard our hearts and minds in Christ Jesus.

And that is the real key – ultimate peace is found in Jesus. Everything else, even good things, cannot replace Jesus. The more we learn to trust that Jesus is the only thing that brings true and lasting peace, the more we will be able to experience comfort, rather than anxiety, in our spirits.

12
Learning to Wait Well

Good morning kids! Today I have a collection of verses. Almost every day I read a little bit from the Psalms because it encourages me the way the Psalmists pour themselves out to God in the midst of their lives, both the good and the bad. One common theme that has stood out to me recently is waiting on the Lord.

5:3 - "I lay my requests before you and wait in expectation"
27:14 - "be strong and take heart and wait for the Lord"
37:34 - "wait for the Lord and keep His law"
130:5 - "I will wait for the Lord, my soul waits, and in His word I put my hope"

One interesting thing I have noticed in looking at the original Hebrew word for "wait" is some translations will say "wait" on the Lord, and some will say "hope" in the Lord, while still others will say "trust" in the Lord. All three of these words are suggested by the same Hebrew word.

In every case, I think the Psalmists believe God hears them, but He might not answer them right away. When we come before God, we will be heard, but He will most likely meet us in ways we aren't expecting. This is why we must wait, and hope, and trust, because He will answer.

I am studying this idea of waiting for the Lord, because I often become discouraged by how much I continue to struggle with the same things; how often I find myself defeated by the same bad attitudes. I feel like I'm not growing enough in my relationship with Jesus, so there must be something wrong with me.

I am thinking, though, this might actually be something very right; this might be how it should feel when we are seeking to know God. That's why the Psalmists repeatedly write about waiting on God.

We need to come before God and reframe our minds to wait patiently, to wait for Him to meet us, and help us to grow, in His time, according to what is best for us. We have to let go of our expectations that God will do what we want, when we want it. As it says in The Lion the Witch and the Wardrobe, Aslan is not a tame lion, but He is good. He will meet us on His terms. We just need to learn how to wait well.

<u>13</u>
Waiting Expectantly

Good morning kids! I'm continuing with some more thoughts on waiting. Today's verses are Isaiah 40:29-31:

"He gives power to the weak and strength to the powerless. Even youths will become weak and tired, and young people will fall in exhaustion. But those who wait for the LORD will find new strength. They will soar high on wings like eagles. They will run and not grow weary. They will walk and not faint."

Isaiah was prophesying about the Israelites who would be exiled in Babylon. In the beginning of this chapter, he was reminding them God is all powerful. Even when they would be in exile, God would still be all-powerful and all-knowing and abounding in perfect love. They needed to be reminded of this often because they forgot easily.

We forget easily too. Our world and idols may look different than theirs, but our minds and our weak faith are the same. We often feel tired and weak in our lives. We also despair and turn to idols, to false gods. We seek relief in lies rather than waiting for the Lord.

We need to remember, though, God is still with us, even in these places. He allows us to feel this weakness so we can realize He alone is able to be our true strength.

Strong emotions and feelings will often come and go, leaving us confused and exasperated, but we are called to wait for God in these times. And it is not just a quiet waiting for nothing. This same phrase can be translated as "those who hope in God." This means we are hopeful that He is faithful and loving while we wait expectantly for Him to show up.

After we have waited expectantly for Him, He will eventually renew our strength. Our spirits will soar like eagles. We will run and not get tired.

It is the patient waiting that allows us to understand and appreciate the real strength that comes from God and His love for us, not from ourselves or from this world. It is the waiting that helps us to understand how weak we are by ourselves and how strong we are when we allow Christ to be our strength.

14
Active Waiting

Good morning kids! Here is a third text regarding the idea of waiting for God. Today's verse is James 1:4:

"Let perseverance finish its work so that you may be mature and complete, not lacking anything."

The Bible translators are using the word "perseverance" to translate a word from the original Greek meaning endurance, or a patient and steadfast waiting.

I think James uses a little bit stronger phrase to tell us to wait for God than Isaiah or David did. He says we must persevere, we must patiently wait, because it is the only way in which we can become mature and complete in Christ.

Waiting is an action verb for James. It is not waiting around being bored. It is actively seeking God even when it seems like we're not getting anywhere. Although we are waiting to find God; to experience a deepening relationship with Him; we do not stop seeking. We are steadfastly waiting for Him, fully expecting Him to show up in His own time.

Even though we may not realize it, we are slowly growing into the people God created us to be. Without the waiting and persevering, we cannot discover the full measure of the good things He has in store for us.

15
Training Ourselves to be Godly

Good morning kids! Today's verse is 1 Timothy 4:7:

"Have nothing to do with godless myths and old wives' tales; rather, train yourself to be godly."

This is in the middle of a longer passage of encouragement and instruction to young Timothy from Paul. I've always passed over this verse without considering what it was saying or how it added to the verses that follow.

When I looked deeper into this passage, I found that in the Jewish faith at the time of Timothy, people would often study the sayings of famous rabbis or Jewish myths. These sayings or stories were hypothetical, pertaining to various issues within the Jewish laws.

Paul tells Timothy to have nothing to do with these things, but to train himself in godliness. The term Paul uses for godliness in this verse has to do with having an attitude that seeks to honor and know God. We should train ourselves to seek God with an attitude of reverence.

I think this verse speaks very much to us in the age of social media. So many Christians have misdirected their faith and meditation on quotes from sentimental devotionals that are focused on massaging a sense of self-worth apart from God. Many of these quotes are often sifted from social media accounts that these people follow for inspiration.

Many Christians also draw inspiration from our modern version of "old wives' tales" in the form of short sappy invented stories passed around on social media as if they really happened.

I think modern day Christians have a tendency to gravitate towards these things because it is easy. These quotes and stories show up in their feeds and they think a quick perusal of them while they are in between things counts for a devotional life. It is so much easier than trying to read and understand the Bible...

Instead, these things train us to be spiritually lazy. They increase the likelihood that we will not seek God in the places where He can be found.

Remember, we believe we are in a relationship with the God of the universe. We have access to real truth revealed in scripture and in the living Christ.

<u>16</u>
Gradual Healing

Good morning kids! Today's verses are from Mark 8:22-25:

"When they arrived at Bethsaida, some people brought a blind man to Jesus, and they begged him to touch the man and heal him. Jesus took the blind man by the hand and led him out of the village. Then, spitting on the man's eyes, he laid his hands on him and asked, 'Can you see anything now?' The man looked around. 'Yes,' he said, 'I see people, but I can't see them very clearly. They look like trees walking around.' Then Jesus placed his hands on the man's eyes again, and his eyes were opened. His sight was completely restored, and he could see everything clearly."

There are several interesting things about this miracle. First of all, it is only recorded in the gospel of Mark. It is one of a handful of miracles where the person receiving the healing is not the one seeking Jesus. We are told that some people brought the man to Jesus.

It is interesting that Jesus then proceeds to lead the man outside of the town, away from the crowd. I think He did this so that He could make a personal connection with the man. Since he was brought to Jesus, we could assume he didn't really know much about Him. Jesus will, at times, lead us away from the crowd to make a personal connection, because He wants to be known in a way that is unique to us.

Once they were away from the crowd, Jesus laid His hands on the man's eyes, and the blind man's vision came back a little bit, but it was still blurry. Then Jesus laid His hands on the man's eyes a second time and his vision became completely clear.

It is one of the only miracles with a sort of gradual healing. I think this is how it is with most of us. Jesus heals our pain and the sickness of our sin gradually. When we first come to know Him, it is hard for us to trust Him enough to receive His full healing. We trust Him enough to see things a little better, but they are still blurry.

Jesus gives time for the man's faith to grow. He cared more for his faith than his sight. He let the man experience his healing gradually to strengthen his faith.

It is the same with us. As we continue in our relationships with Jesus, our trust grows and we become more willing to accept His goodness and strength. When we take Jesus' hand and let Him lead us away from the crowds, His healing will steadily go deeper into our hearts and minds, so we come to see things more clearly.

17
Dealing With Discouragement

Good morning kids! Sorry I haven't sent out any morning texts lately. I have had a really difficult time quieting my spirit and mind before God this week. Even after so many years, the attitudes and ideas of the fallen world still war against the Life of Jesus inside me.

As you get older, you will hear many people who don't believe in Jesus saying things about how Christians believe in Jesus because they are weak. They will say people think they need God because they can't handle life on their own.

The opposite is really the case. When Jesus says we must take up our crosses, or whoever wants to find their lives must lose them for His sake, He is calling us to follow Him down the harder road.

He is calling us to deal with the difficulties of our lives directly, with Him. The life of faith never calls us to avoid dealing with hardships. In reality, this is the hard and narrow path that leads to our truest lives.

Jesus says in John 10:10:

"The thief comes only to steal and kill and destroy; I have come that they may have life and have it to the full."

So, in these days, and weeks, and sometimes months, where I struggle to have a faithful heart before God, I have to be diligent to read my Bible and seek Him anyway. I have to get out of my own way. I have to daily repent for the way I allow myself to follow along down the wide road; for the way I let myself believe lies that make me discouraged or angry or hopeless; for making myself vulnerable to attitudes that steal, kill and destroy life in my soul.

Jesus loves us so much that He sacrificed Himself for the opportunity to offer us life to the fullest measure. He is always seeking us, and He always wants to be found by us. If we're not finding Him, it's because we're the ones who have wandered away.

<u>18</u>
The Consolation of God

Good morning kids! Today's verse is 1 Peter 5:10:

"And the God of all grace, who called you to his eternal glory in Christ, after you have suffered a little while, will himself restore you and make you strong, firm and steadfast."

I'm 46 years into this faith journey, and every step of the way I've been riddled by doubt. But God continues to show up.

This Covid quarantine, in particular, has been like a bandage torn from a festering wound exposing my brokenness. In our house, we have all had our moments of inconsolable self-pity, blatant self-righteousness, anger, thinly veiled meanness of spirit, pride, or anxiety.

As for my part in all of this, I'm thinking it is really a blessing. By exposing that wound, that brokenness, it is getting cleansed. It stings, but this is a time where I can sense healing grace. I am reminded from today's verse that all of my doubt and wrong thinking has paved the way for times of God's consolation.

These last few days have been especially difficult, but I really felt like God showed up this morning in all of your voices. It was a rush of grace and mercy, washing some of the infection out of my wounds.

Text Messages to my Children

It was a reminder to me that the times of doubt and struggle, when God seems so unlikely, are actually times of promise. If I just listen, they are promising the consolation of God, because He will always eventually deliver it. Just remember, our sense of His consolation will always come and go, otherwise our faith would be meaningless.

<u>19</u>
Books That Aren't the Bible

Good morning kids! I don't have a verse this morning, but rather a few quotes from CS Lewis that I was reminded of on my run yesterday. I feel like the Holy Spirit whispered these quotes to me out of my memories to help me re-focus on Him at the end of a long week. I have been struggling with feeling not particularly secure in multiple ways.

Everyday started with a "here-we-go-again" sort of a sigh. One problem for me is I often give in to my emotions the instant I wake up. This reminded me of a CS Lewis quote from "Letters to Malcolm: Chiefly on Prayer" that says:

"Relying on God has to begin all over again every day as if nothing had yet been done."

While it is true we are saved once and for all by Jesus, God is renewing us day-by-day. It will take a lifetime of learning to rely on Him each day, over and over again.

The monotonous nature of these Covid quarantine days has especially provided a gracious training ground to learn to let go of control and reframe my reliance on God rather than myself. I think this tendency to rely on myself rather than God, at its roots, has to do with deep issues of pride.

And as I thought about this issue of pride, another quote from Lewis, out of "Mere Christianity," rose up out of my memories:

"As long as you are proud you cannot know God. A proud man is always looking down on things and people: and, of course, as long as you are looking down you cannot see something that is above you."

So, I'm trying to learn to start reframing my reliance, at the start of each day, so I can see what is above me. This can feel exasperating, as if I'm never making any progress. And sometimes it feels a little hopeless. I feel like it is not something that will get better. And then, again, one last Lewis quote bubbled up out of my memory from "Letters to an American Lady" that says:

"There are far, far better things ahead than any we leave behind."

Remember, God loves us perfectly, which means greater joy is always ahead, regardless of our worldly circumstances, if we are learning to love Him better.

While reading the Bible should be a fundamental priority in our lives, it is also good to read other books that encourage us as we seek God. When we read these things, they soak into our minds and spirits. They get filed away when we don't even realize it.

This allows the Holy Spirit to pull them out and offer them to us when we need them, like happened with me on my run yesterday. It helps us to speak truth to ourselves.

20
Life is Holy Ground

Good morning kids! These past few weeks I have not been very successful in living my way into the truth that all of life is holy ground, but I'm trying to remind myself it is still true nonetheless. And that's okay, because this re-orienting of my hopes and values is a slow business, a lifelong journey.

There's a lot of noise in the world, as well as in my own mind, trying to monopolize my attention; trying to convince me that truth and meaning are to be found in the cacophony of popular opinion; that my happiness is totally dependent upon how I navigate through the chaos of a million urgent questions.

But, for the time being at least, I feel a bit of a reprieve coming. Sometimes God brings us out of the wilderness "into a spacious place" (Ps 18:19); into a place where we are able to "be still before the Lord and wait patiently for Him" (Ps 37:7).

I think it is the nature of life that I can only handle limited glimpses of this grace, but each successive moment in these spacious places drives the truth a little deeper into my core, so I'm a little less dominated by circumstances and popular opinion than I was the day before.

All of life is, after all, holy ground.

<u>21</u>
Ultimate Things

Good morning kids! On my customary social distance outing yesterday, I was thinking through all of the things I've been feeling during this past week of Covid quarantine - anxiety, frustration, fear, anger, annoyance.

It struck me how much of my hope I've placed in good things, but not ultimate things. And I was truly disturbed to realize how much of my hope I have placed in outright lies. I have allowed myself to place my hope in created things rather than in the Creator of things.

I suspect I have many ideas about truth I haven't really experienced, that I haven't come to terms with in the actual living of my life. It is a lifelong journey to live those truths into a heart-level understanding; to be able to say, as Paul said in Phil 4:12-13: "I know what is to be in need. I know what it is to have plenty. I have learned the secret of being content in any and every situation, whether well fed or hungry, whether living in plenty or in want."

There are so many terrible things about this Covid pandemic, but it is also so raw that I'm hopeful I might live this experience into an unshakable hope; into a greater joy that is less dependent on my circumstances; that I can distance myself from the lies I am so prone to trust, and experience true things until they permeate my heart and my understanding with the contentment of Christ.

22

47th Birthday Run...and Some Rare Thoughts About Politics

Good morning kids! It was nice to get out for my 47th birthday run in the daylight! Birthdays are a good time to reflect on where we've been and where we're going, so I wanted to share with you some of the thoughts flowing through my mind today.

Not surprisingly, this year was a strange one. I have always had a tendency to get stuck in my own head, and this year gave me lots of opportunities to get way back in there, thanks to the pervasive isolating effects of Covid.

One thing that affected us all, which I have not spoken of personally, was the divisive and contentious election year in the midst of an already confounding pandemic. This was particularly alarming and disheartening to me as a Christian, because it seemed members of the broad church so willingly misrepresented personal political opinions for religious "truth."

I was, and continue to be, discouraged to see Christians informed mostly by their personal opinions, fueled so easily by social media that is almost comically manipulative (and easily disproved), just because it fits with what they want to hear.

This has had a further isolating effect on me personally, because I don't understand how so few Christians seem to be at all informed by the Bible, and, more importantly, by the person of Christ. The Christ these people are often presenting is not the historical Jesus who was crucified.

It is not the Christ spoken of by those first century followers who knew Him, and witnessed His life, and His death – and His inexplicable return to life – first hand.

It is not the Christ whose message those followers spread throughout the ancient Roman Empire, despite the fact it made them all outcasts, minimizing their cultural (and especially political) power.

The first century Christians who personally knew Jesus became, almost without exception, willing martyrs because they witnessed absolute Truth and Power and Goodness and Joy in the historical person of Christ.

It doesn't take much reading in the gospels, or the epistles, to see the total disconnect between the Christianity of the Bible and much of today's Christianity, with its preposterous volume and content of supposed Christian messages flooding across social media, especially as it has concerned the election during this past year.

I love you kids and I want you to remember, being a Christian unites us with other people in the truth of Christ, not in politics or sociological ideologies. Beware of allowing yourselves to get caught up in these divisive arguments that manipulate scripture for worldly purposes.

As we are trying to be involved participants in our society, when we vote our consciences that are informed by our relationships with God, we will often have very different opinions than others who are trying to do the same thing.

Jesus came to save people and invite them into a relationship with Him. He did not come to establish a democratic or republican government, or a capitalist or socialist system.

He came that we might learn to know Him and to experience His love with all of our hearts and souls and minds, and to love our neighbors as ourselves; to love them with the grace and mercy with which He loves us.

23
Somewhere Between Young and Old

Good morning kids! I have a couple of other thoughts I wanted to share that have been going through my head concerning my 47th birthday.

Aside from Covid and the election, another significant challenge for me this year has been grappling with the realization I'm suddenly somewhere between young and old. I kind of thought I'd have things figured out a little better by this time. Instead, I've realized I can't really rely on myself to solve life's riddles and complexities on my own.

And here's the good news, I have been seeking God, through the person of Jesus, for nearly my whole life. Granted, I have derailed and lost my good intentions more times than I can recount. But this year has afforded me the blessing of seeing, more clearly than ever before, how much I have made personal goodness and acceptability before God about me.

I continue to struggle with making the "figuring out of things" about me, with the hope of connecting the disjointed ideas of truth bumping around in my head, all on my own, so I can take credit for it. I continue to fight against relaxing my grip on my life so God can be God.

This realization is, I believe, where God is trying to bring all people, and it doesn't matter if it takes 10 years, or 20 years, or 47 years.

Lately, as I have written about recently, I have been struck by how often Biblical writers talk about waiting for God.

Isaiah 30:15 says, for instance - "In returning and rest is your salvation. In quietness and trust is your strength."

Or one of the many references in the Psalms, 27:14 - "Be strong and take heart and wait for the Lord."

I wonder why it is so important to wait quietly?

I think it is because we are called to be quiet and to focus outside of ourselves on the source of Truth. I am grateful for this year, because I am learning, more than I would have been able to in a regular (more comfortable) year, to wait quietly and expectantly for God to show up.

I am slowly learning I can't make it happen by my own will. But I am growing confident that God is true to His promise in Isaiah 40:31, "Those who wait for the Lord will find new strength. They will soar high on wings like eagles. They will run and not grow weary. They will walk and not faint."

So, despite much turmoil and anxiety throughout my 47th year, I wouldn't trade it, because it has pushed me closer to being who I would want to be, if I were wise enough to desire it.

<u>24</u>
Godliness…With Contentment

Good morning kids! Today's verses are from 1 Timothy 6:6-8:

"Yet true godliness with contentment is itself great wealth. After all, we brought nothing with us when we came into the world, and we can't take anything with us when we leave it. So, if we have enough food and clothing, let us be content."

The search for contentment is at the core of our hearts and minds. The nature of our spirit is to be restless. And so, we are pestered by a nagging sense that we will be more content if only we keep pushing through to the next thing, whatever it is.

So often, we especially equate greater wealth with greater contentment. Paul tells us here, though, that godliness, with contentment, is itself great wealth. Godliness, the way he's using it here, means seeking God with a wholehearted devotion.

It is interesting he doesn't simply say, godliness is great wealth. He says godliness, with contentment, is great wealth. I think he is suggesting it is possible to devote ourselves to God and not be content.

If we cannot be content with knowing God, it is because our hearts and minds are saying "God, you are good, but you are not enough. I would have enough if I could have you AND..." Whatever the AND is, that is the deceptive thing stealing our contentment.

Our society is focused on the AND. It says God is fine, but we need a certain job, or we need to look a certain way, or we need to have certain friends, or we need our family to be a certain way, or we need to have certain kinds of experiences, or we need to buy certain kinds of things, or we need to achieve a certain level of success - then we will be content.

Society tells us it is good to feel this way; that we need to continually strive towards these things; that we should never settle with what we have. This drives the deception deeper, truly twisting our hearts and clouding our minds.

God gave us minds and talents in order to make a meaningful living. He wants us to enjoy and value our friends and families. He even wants us to enjoy the things that we can buy. Paul is not saying we should only seek God and stop doing everything else.

The way the AND twists things is it makes contentment about us. It says, "make me comfortable and give me what I want, God, then I will also devote myself to you." This attitude of trying to use God to make us content according to the world's standards will actually make us discontent and unhappy in the long run.

God wants our contentment to be based on our relationship with Him, not because He's selfish or egotistical, but because He knows the world's suggestion of God AND will divide our souls so we never really find contentment.

Most days, I fail at this. My soul is very much torn between wanting comfort as the world defines it and seeking God with a wholehearted devotion. But I take hope in the very fact that I do feel torn. It is a good indication of God's faithfulness, because it means He is calling me into a deeper relationship with Him. I believe I feel torn because God intends to make me truly content.

And we need to give ourselves some grace, because He does not expect us to seek Him perfectly. He just wants us to be willing to grow in that direction.

25
Guarding Treasures

Good morning kids! I have struggled to have a quiet spirit while I have studied my Bible this week. I have always felt pressure to try and make myself seem really spiritual and intelligent, as if it were my responsibility to create whatever truth or wisdom I might find in the Bible. As always, I tend to put myself first.

This is not to say our role in our spiritual growth isn't important. It is our responsibility to be disciplined enough to open our Bibles and read, but we cannot make ourselves wise. It is God alone who is gracious enough to impart His wisdom to our souls, but only when we make ourselves available.

Today, I felt like I made myself available, but just barely, when I read 2 Timothy 2:14:

"Guard, through the Holy Spirit who dwells in us, the treasure which has been entrusted to *you.*"

My mind was cluttered with a dozen thoughts of what I needed to do today and I was about to close my Bible and move on with the day, when a small voice in my head urged me to look again more closely at this verse I had never underlined before during the dozens of times I had read 2 Timothy in the past. I believe this was the voice of the Holy Spirit.

As I looked more closely, I was struck by how Paul is not simply saying to guard our hearts and/or our minds. He uses greater imagery. We are told to guard the treasure entrusted to us with the help of the Holy Spirit.

We are like a bank vault where God has deposited an incredibly expensive treasure. It is our responsibility to guard it. Fortunately, God has given us help, so we don't have to guard it all by ourselves. Just like a bank uses locks and alarms and sometimes even armed guards, we have the help of the Holy Spirit who lives in us.

For those of us who have accepted the deposit of this treasure, however imperfectly we may understand it, it is our responsibility to preserve and protect it as the basis of our soul's value. We need help to protect it from the worldliness and selfishness surrounding us, threatening to break in and steal it.

It also occurred to me, sometimes I can become too comfortable with this treasure, so I take it for granted. I feel like it is plenty secure, so I don't concern myself with actively guarding it. It is so easy for me to forget I have been entrusted with a precious gift.

From my experience, when I don't watch over this treasure, I quickly become selfish and arrogant in my soul. Although the treasure might be secure within me, when I disregard it, it can be robbed from me nonetheless, as if it is an inside job where I conspire to disarm the security and let the thief in myself.

It is painful to realize how often I fail this responsibility, and can so easily be a poor steward of the treasure God has entrusted to me.

But every day with Jesus is a new day. The Holy Spirit is within us. He is there to help, if only we will accept it. So, today, I will practice refocusing my mind away from all of those urgent things I am so prone to fixate upon, and instead, try to ground myself first in gratitude for the treasure entrusted to me.

26
The Sort of Spirit God Gives Us

Good morning kids! Today's verse is 2 Timothy 1:7:

"For the Spirit God gave us does not make us timid, but gives us power, love and self-discipline."

Paul wrote this second letter to Timothy about four years after the first letter. He had finished all three of his missionary journeys and was now writing Timothy as an old man sitting in a dark Roman prison cell awaiting his death. Many historians believe Paul was beheaded not long after this letter was written.

It is interesting, then, that Paul is not seeking comfort from Timothy. This makes me wonder if Timothy was a more sensitive sort of person; if he was more prone to discouragement than Paul. This gives me a lot of comfort because I struggle to be as strong as Paul often seems in his letters.

I often give in to self-pity, thinking I'll never get past my many weaknesses and short comings. I am easily overwhelmed by the uncertainty of life. I think Timothy was maybe similar to me in this regard.

But Paul doesn't condemn Timothy or criticize him. Paul understands we all have different strengths and weaknesses. So, he encourages Timothy from his prison cell. He reminds

Timothy how God has created all of us who have believed and received the Holy Spirit in our lives.

The spirit God gave us is not timid or cowardly or fearful. If we are feeling afraid, we can be sure this fear is not from God. It is from the part of our hearts that do not trust God. The Spirit God gave us will enable us to be strong, so we can stand up against our fear and follow God's will even when we feel weak.

His Spirit is also a spirit of love, so we will be less prone to self-pity and selfishness because He will give us His love so we will be more and more concerned about God and other people than we are about our own comfort.

Lastly, Paul tells us the spirit God gives us helps us to be self-controlled. In and of ourselves, we tend to be dominated by our selfishness and fear, which is why God shared His Spirit with us, because it gives us the power to be self-controlled when we wouldn't be able to in our own strength alone.

Regardless of how bad we might be feeling, God has already given us a spirit of power and of love and of self-discipline, so take comfort in what God has given us, knowing He will also bring us to a place where we can accept and trust in these gifts.

27
The Refiner's Fire

Good morning kids! My mind has been a little tired through the holidays, so I've mostly just been reading my Bible without any major insights. But even when we're kind of worn down, we still need to be interacting with the Bible, because it will still soak in and speak to our spirits, even though we don't always feel it.

My verse for today is Isaiah 48:10:

"I have refined you, but not as silver is refined. Rather, I have refined you in the furnace of suffering."

Sometimes fire is destructive, like the forest fires that burn in our mountains. Sometimes fire is used to completely consume something, like in an incinerator. And then there is the refiner's fire.

This metaphor is used in many passages throughout the Bible. A refiner's fire is used to heat up precious metals like gold and silver until they melt. When they turn into liquid, the pure gold or silver sink to the bottom, while the impurities rise to the top where they burn off and can be removed by the refiner. When it cools back down, it is purer and more valuable than it was before.

God is our Refiner. We are told He refines us in the furnace of suffering. He does not allow us to suffer in order to burn us up and destroy us. He is refining us because we are treasures. We are more precious than silver and gold, and God wants to purify us, not to cause us pain, but to make us more perfect, more like Him.

The life of seeking God is not easy, and we shouldn't expect it to be. But if we seek God, He will skillfully refine us to be the most whole version of ourselves, like a shining bar of gold that has had every impurity removed.

<u>28</u>
Refining Our Brokenness

Good morning kids! I want to build on yesterday's text about God refining us. It says in Proverbs 25:4: "Remove the dross from the silver, and a silversmith can produce a vessel."

When silver is removed from the ground, it isn't particularly useful. It is essentially a raw and unformed rock. But, as we discussed yesterday, when that rock is given to the refiner, he is able to melt it down in order to remove the dross, or the impurities. After these impurities have been removed, the silver becomes useful.

When silver is refined, it becomes strong and malleable. This means that as the silver cools, a silversmith is able to shape it into a vessel, or an object which can be useful, such as a gleaming sword. This sword is not only useful because of its shape, but is more powerful and unbreakable from also having had the impurities removed by Refiner's fire.

It makes me think of Elrond, in the Lord of the Rings. He takes the shattered pieces from the sword that was broken fighting Sauron in ancient days. The sword was broken, like we are broken, by sin and darkness.

He then heats up the silver and re-forges it. This new sword would become stronger at the broken joints of the old sword when it is reforged in the furnace, and so it would be more perfect and powerful and useful than it was before.

But Elrond was not meant to wield this sword. We learn throughout the narrative that the character, Aragorn, was born to wield this perfected sword, but only after he had become ready to claim his true identity as a king.

God is not only refining us simply to remove our impurities. He is ultimately refining us because He wants to shape us in a unique way so we can fulfill the plan He has for us. God is turning you into people who can know Him in a way perfectly unique to you.

This is part of what our faith is. It is the hope that even when we are suffering or bored or scared, God is quietly refining us into more perfect treasures. He is not only removing our impurities, but He is mending us in the places where we are broken so we will become stronger than we could have been if we had not been broken. He is turning us into people meant to know Him more completely; to live the lives He created us for; to claim our true identities.

29
A (not so good) Form of Godliness

Good morning kids! Today's verses are 2 Timothy 3:2-5:

"For people will love only themselves and their money. They will be boastful and proud, scoffing at God, disobedient to their parents, and ungrateful. They will consider nothing sacred. They will be unloving and unforgiving; they will slander others and have no self-control. They will be cruel and hate what is good. They will betray their friends, be reckless, be puffed up with pride, and love pleasure rather than God. They will act religious, but they will reject the power that could make them godly."

In several areas of Paul's letters, he warns against lists of vices, but in his other letters he is normally speaking about surrounding pagan cultures. He is generally drawing a contrast between the world and the followers of Christ.

This letter, though, seems to be slightly different in that he is giving guidance and encouragement to Timothy on how to pastor his church in Ephesus. I think this list of vices is a warning about how Timothy's church members will be at times.

Verse five tells us these church-goers will act religious but will reject the power of God. Other translations say they will have "a form of godliness, but deny its power." These attitudes and behaviors are subtle. They are not as obvious as we would like to imagine.

Christians are prone to get too comfortable with their faith, sliding into an assumption that they're getting pretty good at this righteous living thing. They can all too easily, and unknowingly, start to reject God's power, which is the only thing able to make them godly in the first place.

These subtle attitudes put the believers at the center of their faith, so they resort to acting religious out of self-interest, rather than out of a desire to honor God. It is the cause of the hypocrisy of Christians we so often see.

Now, having said this, it is easy to slide into an "us and them" duality. I am often guilty of this, and it is an attitude of pride. We need to guard against putting ourselves in the righteous category, while thinking of "all those other" people with condescension.

We are all fallen people, and this is a warning to us. These are attitudes that come naturally to us apart from God. We are prone to slide into superficiality and hypocrisy just as much as any other person. When we make our salvation about our own efforts and our own goodness, we easily lose the humility that enabled us to accept Jesus in the first place.

Rather than looking outside of ourselves to cast judgement, this passage should make us look inside of ourselves. It should make us take an honest inventory. It should make us kneel before God, praising Him for His gracious love each new day, recognizing it is only by His mercy that we can enjoy a right relationship with Him.

<u>30</u>
Faith and Imagination

Good morning kids! I have been thinking this past weekend about imagination. Initially, I was thinking about how a well written fairy tale or fantasy story can often reveal deeper truths about life to readers of any age than more literal language can. I think too many people outgrow fairy tales and become too "grown up" to follow their imaginations where they might lead them.

It is difficult to speak literally about the reality of spiritual life. We often don't have the words to describe the struggles and the truths of spiritual life, so we use metaphors to describe what the spiritual life is like by comparing it to situations or pictures we can imagine.

God has given us the ability to imagine, to make connections between our experiences with stories or pictures, so we can discover His deeper truths and know Him more fully. The Bible uses countless metaphors to help us understand who God is and how our relationship with Him should be: God is light; Jesus is the vine; He is living water. And then consider Jesus's parables. Many metaphors run throughout the entire Bible. They help us to connect threads of truth from the Old Testament, through to Christ, and then to the early church of the New Testament.

Currently, I am reading Paul's final letter to Timothy, written shortly before he would be killed. He says in 2 Timothy 4:7:

"I have fought the good fight, I have finished the race, I have kept the faith."

In this metaphor, Paul compares our spiritual lives to running a race. Having run many races, this image really resonates with me. Our life is like a long race, truly like an ultramarathon.

Sometimes, when we study our Bibles, we come across ideas that are especially interesting to us, like this race metaphor is to me. I think it is good in these times to stop and dig down deep and see what treasures we might discover there. So, I will be parked in this place for a bit to share what sorts of connections my imagination is able to make between life with Christ and running a race.

31
Relentless Forward Progress

Good morning kids! This morning I want to look again at 2 Timothy 4:7:

"I have fought the good fight, I have finished the race, I have kept the faith."

Paul spoke several times of life as a race. Rather than being in the midst of the race, in this verse he says he has finished the race. Indeed, he would be executed not long after this letter by the Roman emperor, Nero.

The word he used for "finished" did not simply mean he had reached the end of the race. It is a Greek word suggesting that in completing the race, he fulfilled his purpose. He accomplished what was set out for him.

God gives each of us a course to race, sort of like the mountain ultramarathons that I race. They ascend and descend mountains, sometimes on difficult rocky trails, and sometimes on smooth and fast trails. Sometimes the trails follow lush and shaded streams, and other times they climb arid, dusty and sun-scorched hillsides.

Ultramarathons are long enough that, in every single one I have run, I have experienced exuberant joy and overwhelming discouragement, and everything in between, along the way from the start to finish.

The key to ultramarathons, though, and the key to the life of following Jesus, is to keep moving forward. Some people describe ultramarathons as "relentless forward progress." The pace doesn't really matter. The important thing is we are relentless about moving forward.

Paul had finished his race by continually moving forward. And the feeling of finishing an ultra is always a feeling of accomplishment, regardless of how you place, because each racer has completed the course set out for them. They have each pushed through the unique difficulties that faced them during their races. They finished, in spite of wrong turns, bloody knees, cramping muscles, or sick stomachs. They stayed the course to the end.

Being faithful in living life with Christ also means we just need to stay on the course to the best of our ability. There will be low points along the way, but He has promised to take us to completion.

You kids are each on your own course. It is going somewhere special and unique to you. You may not know where the course is going, or what hills and valleys lie ahead. You are only called to be faithful to keep trying to move forward, to keep looking for Jesus in the place you are right now.

He's not miles away from you. He's marking the course just ahead, and it is going somewhere you have the strength to go to, a place you will find uniquely satisfying. Just keep moving forward towards the next course marker that you can see right now.

32
Running Our Own Courses

Good morning kids! I want to return to the metaphor of running a race again this morning. When Paul uses this metaphor in Philippians, he says in 3:14:

"I press on toward the goal to win the prize for which God has called me heavenward in Christ Jesus."

While we are all running in this ultramarathon of life, we are not all on the exact same course. Paul says he was pushing towards the goal God had specifically called him to. And God has called each of us, individually, to complete a course unique to us as well; to take hold of a prize He has reserved for us alone.

It is difficult to see this, because from the moment we are born, the world is telling us we are actually all running the same race. It encourages us to root our sense of worth and accomplishment in comparison to other people. It tells us we are actually racing against one another in every facet of our lives. This is one of the great dangers of social media; one of the ways it contributes to the epidemic of depression and anxiety in the world today.

Social media encourages us to invite the subtle spirit of envy into our hearts, so we desire to be where other people are, enjoying the things those other people have. It quietly nudges us to become unhappy and discouraged with where we are in our own personal races.

The world tells us not to settle; that we must always strive for more. Not more of Jesus, though. Always more of us. More for us.

Paul also encourages us to always strive to move forward, but he is calling us to strive to pursue Jesus; to know more of Him, so we can be transformed in our hearts and minds to be more like Him. When our self-worth is rooted in the person of Jesus, envy is replaced by peace, by contentment.

The world's race plays on our sense of entitlement. It tells us we need to "get what we deserve." When we are fooled into making the race about ourselves, about our own glory and comfort, we become easily disheartened, because the world's race is distorted by our tendency towards pride, envy, jealousy, greed and selfishness.

This is not the course God has laid out for us. When we step onto the course God has called us to, Jesus becomes the goal, and when we strive to know Him, He transforms our work and our relationships. He infuses them with meaning and purpose and contentment, because we are on the courses He created us to run upon, where He alone is our prize.

33
Racing in the Present Moment

Good morning kids! I am still thinking about Paul's metaphor of the life of faith in God as a race. In the Philippians passage, he says in 3:12-13:

"Not that I have already obtained all this, or have already arrived at my goal, but I press on to take hold of that for which Christ Jesus took hold of me. Brothers and sisters, I do not consider myself yet to have taken hold of it. But one thing I do: Forgetting what is behind and straining toward what is ahead."

At first reading, it seems like Paul is saying we shouldn't live in the past, but we should focus on the future.

When I hold this metaphor up to my experience of running ultramarathons, this conclusion seems to fit. It is a waste of energy to keep looking over my shoulder at what is behind me. I have to focus my energy on moving forward; on getting to what is ahead as efficiently as possible; on getting to the finish line.

But when I think more closely about running a race, in order to move forward, we need to live in the present, in the here and now. And I think Paul would agree that, in straining toward what is ahead, we must first be aware of the present.

God meets us in the present. God told Moses He is "I am." And Jesus also told His followers, before Abraham was, "I am."

God doesn't say, "I was," or "I will be." He says, "I am."

We must be rooted in our present reality as we strive forward to know the Truth of God in Jesus. Just as in a race, I am pushing myself forward towards the goal by being present in each step. To make forward progress, I have to navigate the rocks and roots, the curves and hills, where I am at that moment. It is no good thinking so much about the future that I trip over the rock right in front of me.

Also, when I race, I have to be aware of my nutrition and hydration in the present moment. Many times, I have become so focused on the future, on finishing as fast as possible, on how great it would be to achieve a podium finish, that I have forgotten to take in any calories or fluids for several miles. And I am suddenly reduced to a hazy, led-footed trudge.

We need to relate to God in the here and now. By being present before Jesus, He is able to help us navigate the tricky footing in our lives today. We need to reach out to Him in our current circumstances. He can nourish us and replenish us. He can give us the energy to keep moving forward.

When Paul tells us to forget what is behind, he doesn't mean we should be oblivious to our past. We should remember both our past failures and our past successes, our bad memories and our happy memories. They should all remind us of God's faithfulness, so we can have confidence in the steps we are taking today.

But we should not be preoccupied with the past. We should not stop in the middle of the trail and stare back at what is behind us. Focusing too intently on our past failures, and even on our past successes, paralyzes us in the present.

It can make it impossible to go forwards because we're pointing backwards.

Keep straining for what lies ahead with the God who is here today. Seek Him in what is happening today. Consider how He has been there in the past, so it can help us to look for the ways He is showing up today, and then strain towards the promises God has in store for us up ahead on the trails we are running.

34
God's Megaphone

Good morning kids! I have been thinking about fear lately. It is something I have thought about often over the past few years because it has become more and more clear to me I have allowed fear to control me throughout my entire 30 years of adult life.

I share this with you because I take you seriously as equals in Christ. I am only a few years ahead of you in this life, and the best thing I can give you is my honesty regarding how I am experiencing things. I don't want you to look back and have the misperception that life came easily for me, or that I was better than I actually was.

So, this fear of mine is something I mostly avoid talking about, because I often don't even know what I'm afraid of. I'm not sure where it came from, and I often can't even really describe it.

It is just a general and perpetual dread that I will eventually make a mess of everything in my life. Sometimes I am distracted from this by the many good things in my life, like the frequent joy of sharing life with all of you.

But it always comes back.

I don't think this particular psychological shortcoming is common to everyone. It may not be something any of you will experience in your lives. But I want you to know it has been somewhat crippling to me.

I was encouraged today to notice Psalm 53:5, where King David says of the Israelites, "But there they are, overwhelmed with dread, where there was nothing to dread."

I love how the Bible is full of imperfect people we can relate to in our particular weaknesses. It makes me realize we should not discount our struggles as if they are stupid, or as if they don't matter, or as if we should just bottle them up and never share them.

When we share our struggles, even when they don't make any sense to us, I believe God is pleased. I believe He is listening. And I believe it is opening up a channel for Him to show us His love, to meet us in those broken places.

CS Lewis said in his book, "The Problem of Pain," that pain is God's megaphone to rouse a deaf world. It is the Holy Spirit speaking to us in our struggles. It is our nature to live with all sorts of pain and shame and shortcomings. And in a way, it is a blessing. Without them we would never want to know God.

35
Perfect Love Drives Out Fear

Good morning kids! I want to wrap up some of my thoughts on my struggle with fear. For me and my fear, I am always reminded of 1 John 4:18:

"Such love has no fear, because perfect love expels all fear. If we are afraid, it is for fear of punishment, and this shows that we have not fully experienced his perfect love."

This verse seems straightforward in my mind. But the thing that expels fear is the experience of God's love in our hearts, not the perception of the idea in our minds. Consequently, I will continue to struggle with fear to the degree I reject the experience of His perfect love in my heart. I continue to fear punishment for all of the poor choices I make; for all of the ways I fall short by my own power.

I think this is because I easily manipulate the possibility of God's perfect love for self-serving ends. In my self-centeredness, I pursue an imperfect form of love that is not love at all. It is narcissism.

My mistaken perception of love easily reverts to the world's perspective. It is a perspective that love is only experienced in a reciprocal way; that love is reliant on what I do. It says, "If I do THIS, then I will get THAT."

The problem with this view is, more often than not, I don't do "THIS," so how can I ever expect to get "THAT." I know I don't deserve to be rewarded. I really deserve to be punished. And so, I am afraid.

But God's love is perfect. It is about Him and the unconditional, sacrificial love of Jesus. It is not about my goodness or my efforts. God is calling me to experience this unconditional love. This love drives away all fear because it understands the punishment we deserve was already borne by Christ.

36
Introspection vs. Reflection

Good morning kids! One of the reasons I send these texts is to continually encourage you to make a habit of reading your Bibles. I know this can be overwhelming, though, because it is a big book and we are often unsure of where to begin to read it. Let me reassure you, though, there is not a right or wrong way to do this.

For me, I don't have much structure in how I read my Bible. I don't always read in a particular order. The important thing, to me, is simply to start each day somewhere in my Bible. With my personality, if I try to incorporate too much structure, it can paralyze me. It tends to shift my focus from seeking Jesus to just checking off a box for completing my Bible reading for the day.

Lately, I have been thinking about the idea of introspection, because I am naturally predisposed to become absorbed by it. I have been this way since I was a child. I am sometimes concerned it is wrong for me to be so introspective. So, when I opened my Bible today, I was looking for verses about introspection.

Two verses I settled on and have been toggling between today are Haggai 1:5:

"Now this is what the Lord Almighty says: 'Give careful thought to your ways.'"

And Lamentations 3:40:

"Let us examine our ways and test them, and let us return to the Lord."

I think "introspection" is often confused with "reflection." It is as if you are leaning over a still mountain lake gazing at the water. Reflection is like looking at the image of yourself and the surrounding mountains. You are considering how things appear reflected on the surface.

Introspection, though, is not merely reflecting on things. It goes deeper. Introspection goes below the surface. It is as if we are trying to look through the images on the surface to see what is happening beneath the surface, to see the fish swimming between the rocks and channels of the lake.

In both of the verses above, God is calling us to be introspective, to look into our hearts, to consider carefully the things we do and why we do them. And this is where I can get trapped.

Sometimes I dive beneath the surface and start to drown. I can easily become totally preoccupied with what is happening in the deeper waters of my heart.

I often try to understand it according to worldly psychology, which is often all about me and how I should define myself. This is what was happening in Haggai. God instructed the people to be introspective, to consider their ways. He would go on to say, if they did so, they would discover they were preoccupied with themselves, all the while ignoring God.

Lamentations also tells us to be introspective; to look into our hearts; to test why we think the way we do, and why we do the things we do. But he doesn't stop there.

He adds the key ingredient to introspection when He says to return to the Lord. He is saying to look into our hearts, and instead of becoming preoccupied with ourselves, we need to become preoccupied with who God is calling us to be.

He is calling us to look into our hearts and turn them towards who Jesus is; to consider how He intends to transform us. This sort of introspection affirms our life in Christ. It makes us into fish who can swim through the deep waters.

<u>37</u>
Drifting With the Tide

Good morning kids! Today I am looking at Hebrews 2:1:

"So we must listen very carefully to the truth we have heard, or we may drift away from it."

It is important to our faith that we regularly engage our minds in the truth that originally brought us to faith in God. The main way we do this is by studying our Bibles, but it could also be doing things like listening to sermons or podcasts or by reading books that speak truth to us.

The writer of Hebrews says we must listen carefully to the truth. If we are not careful to focus on who Jesus is, and who He is calling us to be, the writer says we might drift away.

I like this image of drifting away. It is not sudden. It is not even deliberate. It is simply subtly drifting along like an ocean tide.

When I was in high school, during the summers I would go bodysurfing almost every day. My favorite beach was in a town called Del Mar. I liked it because it extended over a couple of miles, so it was easy to keep space from other people.

I also liked it because the ground under the waves was fairly flat, so when I caught a good wave, I could ride it for a long time without crashing into the sand on the beach.

Because it was flatter, the waves started to break further out from the beach. I had to wear swimming fins on my feet, because I couldn't touch the ground under the water out where the waves started to break.

Some days, when the waves were good, I would be out for hours riding waves in, and swimming back out, without ever touching the sand.

On these days, I felt like I was going back-and-forth in the same spot I had started from. I wouldn't pay very close attention to where I started from because there was no danger of drifting into piers or rocks.

So, when a few hours had passed and I decided to finally swim in to go home, I would always be surprised to find how far I had drifted down the shore. Contrary to my perception, I was not actually swimming in and out in a straight perpendicular line.

Throughout the day, I was unknowingly drifting to the south a few inches at a time, so I would end up a full mile or more down the shore, far from the street where I had parked and gotten into the water at the beginning of the day.

This is what the writer of Hebrews is talking about. This is an image of our spiritual lives. At some point, when we decide to follow Jesus, we swim out into the ocean of faith.

As we kick our way out away from the shore, we need to orient ourselves by engaging our minds in our faith each day.

When we get lazy about this, or allow our busy lives to prevent us from finding any time, we can slowly drift away without even knowing it.

Over the past thirty years, I have had entire years where I looked like I was "living a Christian life," but my mind was not engaged in my faith. I was carelessly drifting away along the tides of worldly concerns.

Despite being redeemed in Christ, I will continue to be at risk of carelessly drifting away for the rest of my life, because I still have a selfish, sinful nature. This is one of the reasons why I am so grateful for you kids and the opportunity to send you these texts, because it encourages me to listen more carefully each morning to the truth I have heard with the hope of passing it along to you.

38
Spiritual Weather

Good morning kids! In the spiritual life there is all sorts of weather, just as in the physical world. There are clear days and cloudy days; seasons of droughts and monsoons; sweltering heat waves and frigid cold fronts. These past couple of weeks, I have been wandering around in a bit of a spiritual fog.

Regarding physical weather, I actually love foggy days, because they are so rare in the mountains. When I'm running through the mountains in the fog, I am never in a hurry. I'm more intent on observing the way the landscape is different. I can only see what is immediately around me, while the horizon fades indistinctly into the surrounding mist. It even absorbs the noise into a peaceful stillness.

I am noticing this week, however, I don't appreciate spiritual fog the same way I do physical fog. When I'm in a spiritual fog, I don't feel desperate or discouraged. I actually feel relatively peaceful, but I just can't focus. It feels as if insight is just beyond reach somewhere on the edge of the mist. As I read my Bible or other books, as I look for topics to send to you kids, I find that my mind has quietly wandered off without my noticing.

In the past, when I have gotten into these sorts of fogs, I have always assumed it's because I'm doing something wrong. I feel like I need to concentrate harder. I think I need to meditate on God with greater focus, as if I could crack some secret code to walk in the bright bluebird sunshine of God's presence at all times without ever seeing a single cloud.

I'm thinking today, though, this is the sort of spiritual weather David was experiencing in places like Psalm 62:5 when he wrote:

"My soul, wait in silence for God alone, for my hope is from Him."

In this passage, David is not fleeing from enemies or wandering in deserts or hiding in caves. He's just waiting in a silent fog putting his hope in God, not in his own ability to try to break through the fog.

God is calling us to adopt an attitude of willingness in our spiritual lives. He is calling us to wait on Him always, to be available for moments of the unexpected grace He has for us, just as I make myself available for moments of grace by just being present in the physical fog.

In spiritual fog, though, I tend to have an attitude of willfulness. I make it my responsibility to break through the fog, to grasp at spiritual insights.

When I am willful, I am actually closing myself off to God's grace. I am making my spiritual life all about me and the delusion that I can focus my own mind and find spiritual truth by my own power. I am tromping off into the fog, thinking I will burn it off by my sheer effort when, in reality,

I don't even know if I'm going north or south. This sort of willfulness is dangerous. It is why I so easily get myself lost.

The weather in our spirit always changes, just as the regular weather. The fog will always eventually lift. But God does not change, and He is teaching us to hope in Him alone in every season. He is calling us towards the sort of willingness that will enable us to be present before Him regardless of the forecast.

39
The Pioneer of Our Salvation

Good morning kids! Today I was reading Hebrews 2:10 where it says:

"In bringing many sons and daughters to glory, it was fitting that God, for whom and through whom everything exists, should make the pioneer of their salvation perfect through what he suffered."

I think it's a little puzzling that it says God made Jesus perfect through His suffering. There are many verses about us being refined and made perfect through our suffering, but the idea is that the fire of suffering is burning off our dross, removing our impurities. Jesus, however, had no impurities to refine.

It says earlier in the verse that God was making Jesus the pioneer of our salvation. The word translated here as "pioneer" is only used four times in the New Testament. In some versions of the Bible, it is translated as "author." Some others translate it as "captain." It seems the idea the original Greek had in mind was that of "a perfect leader."

I especially like the translation "captain" because captains are leaders who journey through the suffering of warfare with their troops. They lead the way through every hardship, not from a distant hill, but from the mud-soaked ground of the trenches with their troops.

It says at the beginning of the verse, God wants to bring His sons and daughters to glory, or to salvation. He knows we cannot get there without someone to lead us. This is why it says it was fitting for God to make Jesus perfect through what He suffered.

We do not follow a God who is far off. We follow a God who was willing to come walk along our paths and through our hardships. He can sympathize with us because He has experienced human life.

He can lead us because He has followed the path without straying. Jesus' character was always perfect, and He was made into the perfect leader; the perfect captain; the perfect pioneer; who could show us the way to salvation because He walked the path of a human life, enduring every hardship faithfully.

<u>40</u>
Singing a New Song

Good morning kids! I have been listening to the 3000 or so songs I have downloaded onto my phone alphabetically for the past month or so (I'm part way through the "G's"). I was thinking it's amazing people continue to write good and fresh sounding songs. I was wondering if we will ever come to a place where there are no more new songs to write.

This got me thinking about the Psalms and the many places where the writers encourage us to sing new songs. In Psalm 96:1, the writer says:

"Sing to the Lord a new song; sing to the Lord, all the earth."

This passage is interesting because he calls all the earth to sing a new song to the Lord, not just the Israelites. He is prophesying the coming of Jesus, who will unite all the earth in Him. Jesus is the new song for all the earth.

Jesus is the new song in each of our lives too. Elsewhere, in Psalm 40:3, David says:

"He put a new song in my mouth, a hymn of praise to our God."

Jesus is not just the new song for all the earth, He is the new song God has given each of us personally. He has put Him in our mouths – almost like food – like the bread of life.

When we receive His gift, we learn to sing new songs to Him because we are all unique in how we relate to Him. Each of our songs are a bit different from one another, so that our very lives become new songs. And as we grow closer to Him, He gives us more new songs only we can sing.

You kids are all beautiful songs that bring such amazing new harmonies and melodies into the lives of your family and friends. I hope you all hear some new and inspiring notes today that will add to the songs your lives are!

41
The Lord Looks at the Heart

Good morning kids! Today I want to look at the beginning of the story of David. God told Samuel one of the sons of Jesse would be king, so Samuel went to Jesse and Jesse presented seven of his sons to Samuel. He had an eighth son too, David, who was tending the sheep, but Jesse didn't mention him.

After God rejected the first seven brothers, Jesse seemed almost embarrassed to even mention David. By the world's standards, David was not as impressive as his seven brothers. The oldest brother seemed to be the very most impressive, but we are told:

"The LORD said to Samuel, 'Don't judge by his appearance or height, for I have rejected him. The LORD doesn't see things the way you see them. People judge by outward appearance, but the LORD looks at the heart.'

It is so difficult, growing up in the fallen world, to not judge ourselves by our appearance or height. We also judge ourselves by how smart we are, or how talented we are in our activities, or how skilled we are at our jobs, or by how nice our things are, or how fit we are, or by how nice our clothes are.

The problem with the way we judge ourselves, though, is we will feel like failures if we get a bad grade, or have a bad performance, or don't get a promotion, or gain weight, or if we can't afford the nicest things.

This is the way the world sees things, and it is an impossible standard intended to make us unhappy and discontent.

But the Lord doesn't see things the way we see things. The Lord looks at our hearts.

David was not perfect. He had many significant failures, but we know from the Psalms that He loved God. He was ultimately more concerned about knowing God than he was about measuring up to the world's standards. And fortunately for all of us, this is really what God is looking for.

42
Our Identities

Good morning kids! In my last text, I wrote about how God looks at our hearts, rather than our outward appearance or performance. Our hearts reveal where we have placed our identities.

Last week I was talking with M, and she had said she likes 1 John 3:1, which says:

"See how very much our Father loves us, for he calls us his children, and that is what we are! But the people who belong to this world don't recognize that we are God's children because they don't know him."

We are told more specifically in Hebrews 2:11 how we actually came to be the children of God:

"So now Jesus and the ones he makes holy have the same Father. That is why Jesus is not ashamed to call them his brothers and sisters."

By taking on a body, Jesus allowed us to become His sisters and brothers. It is as if we were adopted into His family, so His Father became our Father. By Jesus' sacrifice we became the children of God. This is our identity.

The world, though, encourages us to turn our hearts to the things of the world. It tells us to base our identities on other things. It says we are students, dancers, singers, actors, mothers and fathers, runners, employees, husbands and wives – and the list goes on and on. The world tells us these roles are our identities.

These are all good things, but they are gifts from God intended for our enjoyment, and also to help us grow in our character. He wants us to do them well. He does not, however, want them to become our whole identity, because they are fragile and temporary.

Athletes will age. They could become injured, causing their speed and agility to diminish. Sometimes we get a low grade even though we tried our best. Or we work really hard and don't achieve a professional goal. Even with people, at times we will fail in our relationships, or other people will disappoint us.

These activities and relationships give great meaning to our lives, but if they are our whole identity, we will ultimately be disappointed.

God has made us His children, and anchoring our identities in that reality is how He intends us to identify ourselves, because that is where He has hidden our greatest joy. This identity is strong and permanent.

The longer we live, although our bodies will break down, we will only grow more confident in our identities. We will become more and more sure we are the sisters and brothers of Jesus. We will know that, at the end of all things, we are the children of God. That is what we are!

43
Our Portion

Good morning kids! Today I want to look at Psalm 16:5:

"LORD, you alone are my portion and my cup; you make my lot secure."

When David is talking about his "portion," his "cup," his "lot"; he is talking about his inheritance, or what he has taken ahold of for his own. Much of the Old Testament centers around the Israelites and God's promise to give them the inheritance of a land flowing with milk and honey.

But we mostly see them divided, conquered, and displaced as they fail to seek God.

The Israelites ultimately misunderstood God's promises, thinking their inheritance was going to be a place, but David saw their inheritance was actually a person, and God alone was his portion.

We easily believe the lie that the things we have are ours, but nothing really belongs to a person if it can be taken away. We may have some things today, but since we cannot guarantee we will not lose them tomorrow, they are ultimately not really ours. It would be foolish to say any physical thing is our portion, or our lot, because it could become someone else's tomorrow.

The only thing that can really be ours is something that passes into our souls.

For this reason, God has given us His Spirit, through Jesus, so we are able to become His children. By this gift, we are able to claim Him as our portion; as our inheritance. Nothing can take Him out of our souls.

It is as if your soul is a plain white shirt dipped into a richly colored dye. The colors pass into and saturate every part of the fabric, becoming a permanent part of the shirt.

God alone is our portion. He has poured Himself into our souls, saturating our innermost selves with the permanent dye of the Holy Spirit.

<u>44</u>
God Before Us / God Beside Us

Good morning kids! I have been in Psalm 16 for more than a week now. I just can't move past it because every day I am seeing new insights and images from it. The Bible is like that. If you will read it patiently, God will sometimes show up in extraordinary ways.

Today I am looking at Psalm 16:8:

"I have set the LORD always before me. Because He is at my right hand, I will not be shaken."

I love this image of setting the Lord before us. It reminds us we always have the choice to look towards Him, or to aim at Him.

By keeping Him in our line of sight, we are less likely to lose our way, even if we are sailing through dark and choppy waters. If we don't set the Lord before us, we will likely aim at other things that will almost certainly take us away from where we want to be going.

We are also told He is at our right hand, which is a position of power in our lives. When God is at our right hands, He will give us support, counsel and encouragement.

When we point towards God and rely on His support, it doesn't always mean we will be removed from hard times. We often assume God is there to deliver us from difficulties, when in fact He might actually intend for us to move through those situations. He wants us to learn He is faithful; that He is at our right hand so we will not be shaken in those places.

It is as if we are an old wooden sailing ship on stormy seas at night. God is like the lighthouse shining out from the cliffs before us.

We cannot risk trying to go to shore, given the rough seas and the darkness, but if we look ahead towards the lighthouse, we can keep our bearings and avoid crashing into the rocks along the shoreline.

God is also like the anchor we drop deep into the solid ground beneath us as we wait out the stormy night. Our anchor holds us steady, although waves crash against us, and stormy winds try to blow us out into the darkness.

Sometimes God takes us through difficult waters, but He is always there before us if we will look up. And Jesus is also at our right hand to keep us steady through the circumstances we encounter.

45
Waiting For the Morning Light

Good morning kids! I have been silent for a while. The life of the mind and spirit, in my experience, is not constant. There are times when I read my Bible and my mind is quiet. My spirit is not moved.

The important thing is to keep showing up, because God continues to be God, and we need to learn to seek Him regardless of how we feel.

It is a tremendous blessing when we are inspired and encouraged in our meditation on God and His Word, but it is also a blessing that God gives us the opportunity to orient ourselves towards Him in silence, when we don't feel moved, apart from emotion.

These times are necessary for our humility, so we don't fall into thinking we create closeness with God by our own efforts. God is always near to us regardless of how we feel. He is always present in the way we need Him to be. He is teaching us to be faithful.

It says in Psalm 30:5:

"For His anger lasts only a moment, but His favor lasts a lifetime; weeping may remain for a night, but rejoicing comes in the morning."

There will be storms. There will also be long, overcast days where we just want to lay on our beds staring at the ceiling. But God's favor lasts a lifetime.

Eventually Joy comes in the morning. Darkness never lasts forever, whether it's a scary darkness or a lonely darkness or just a silent darkness. Morning light will always follow the nighttime, beaming joy across the landscape of our spirits.

<u>46</u>
Traps and Snares

Good morning kids! I have been looking this past week at the places in the Psalms where it talks about people laying traps, digging pits, or hiding nets that their enemies might step into. Oftentimes, the Psalmists appeal to God that these enemies will fall into the very traps they have laid with their own hands. I've been thinking about how these passages might apply to me.

Many Christians interpret these verses in a very "us versus them" way, as if all of the people outside the church are their enemies. They paint a picture of themselves as faithful believers, appealing to God to protect them from the traps being laid by the great host of corrupt unbelievers all around them.

But, to me, this seems like a highly simplistic, self-righteous interpretation. Our society enjoys broad religious liberties. We mostly live comfortable, prosperous and safe lives, especially compared to the Israelites the writers were addressing.

We could also read the enemy in these passages as Satan laying traps for us, but it breaks down a bit when it talks about the enemy falling into his own traps.

When I read the Psalms and they talk about enemies, rather than the world or Satan, I think of the enemy as the willfulness in my own heart. I think of my own sinfulness.

That is the thing keeping me from the shelter of God's protective wings.

Psalm 7:15 especially captures this idea when it says:

"Whoever digs a hole and scoops it out falls into the pit they have made."

In my own willfulness, I all too often dig self-destructive pits that I will fall into myself.

This is not God punishing us. It is the nature of sin that it sets in motion its own punishments. God is not out there waiting for us to fall so He can condemn us, as so many atheists joke.

God has created a moral universe which nearly everyone believes in, especially the modern educated atheists. Modern secularism is largely built upon a moral platform with the assumption that all reasonable people will agree with its tenets.

Rather than laughing at our blunders, I think it actually breaks God's heart when we fall into the pits that we continually make in our own rebellion against His goodness.

It is also a sign of His great mercy that sin leads to its own punishment, because our failures eventually create the humility that we need to cling to and rest in His perfect love for us.

<u>47</u>
Expectations

Good morning kids! In Psalm 33:16-18 the writer says:

"No king is saved by the size of his army; no warrior escapes by his great strength. A horse is a vain hope for deliverance; despite all its great strength it cannot save. But the eyes of the Lord are on those who fear Him, on those who hope in His unfailing love."

The Psalmist is not saying it is bad to have a large army with mighty warriors and strong battle horses. Just like these kings, we order our lives to be successful in our own battles, to achieve our own goals. God expects us to use our resources to be prepared for our endeavors.

What happens to most of us, though, is we attach our hearts to these plans for success. We develop a rigid spirit of expectation. We expect to get exactly what we want if we do the right things.

At some point we all fall into a lie that essentially says, "Thanks, God, for the tools, I'll take it from here." We place our hope in our plans rather than God.

What we will find is, even when we get what we thought we wanted, in the long run we will be disappointed. Expectations centered on ourselves, apart from God, end up in despair.

Saint Augustine recognized this tendency in himself. He said, "You have made us for yourself, O Lord, and our hearts are restless until they rest in you." When we hope, as the Psalmist said, "in His unfailing love," our hearts will find rest. They will find joy.

When our hearts are transformed to hope in God, as they were created to do, we will naturally release our rigid expectations.

In verses 20-22, the Psalm ends by saying:

"We wait in hope for the Lord; He is our help and our shield. In Him our hearts rejoice, for we trust in His holy name. May your unfailing love rest upon us, O Lord, even as we put our hope in you."

When our hearts hope in God, our only expectation is that we will eventually find God's unfailing love, regardless of our circumstances. Our hearts will find the love and contentment they desired all along.

<u>48</u>
Goodness and the Rich Young Ruler

Good morning kids! I have been thinking a lot about the story of the rich young ruler the past couple of weeks. I can't summarize my thoughts in one text, so I'll look at different parts in separate texts.

To refresh your memory, the story is recounted in Matthew, Mark and Luke. This man came up to Jesus (Mark says he fell on his knees before Jesus) and asks what he must do to get eternal life.

Jesus told him he must follow the Ten Commandments. The man says he had done this since he was a boy.

Mark added an interesting detail, "Jesus looked at him and loved him." He then told the man to sell everything he had, give it to the poor, so his treasure would be in heaven, and then to follow Him.

The young man walked away discouraged because he had much wealth.

This incident is so interesting to me because I think this young man is very similar to the people in our society. In many ways, I relate to him and sympathize with him.

This man was not a social outcast seeking Jesus to save him from sickness or demon possession or any other misfortune. He had a comfortable life.

Moreover, he was moral. Based on what he tells Jesus, we can assume he had come by his wealth honestly, that he had conducted himself honorably, and that he was well respected in his community.

Evangelical churches in the United States are full of such people as this rich young ruler.

Then the young man fell before Jesus and called Him "good teacher." This is the way most people prefer to think of Jesus, even most Christians, if they are honest. The young man thought he was addressing Jesus with a respectful greeting. But Jesus, as He so often does, turned this into a question.

He said, "Why do you call me good? No one is good – except God alone."

This response is puzzling. If I were the young man, I would immediately wonder if Jesus was suggesting He wasn't good. But I think this is exactly the point.

Many of the unclean people begged Jesus, "LORD, if you are willing, you can make me clean." They recognized Jesus was much more than a good teacher. The low and despised people recognized they were in the presence of God, while the high and respected young man thought he was only in the presence of a good teacher.

As people become increasingly confident in their own

goodness, their conception of Jesus becomes more and more that was mainly a good and righteous teacher.

In reality, though, no one will ever be intrinsically good, including ourselves. It is only Jesus who makes us good, not because He was a good teacher, but because He is God.

49
Reformation vs. Transformation

Good morning kids! The next thing I want to look at in the story of the rich young ruler is the question he poses to Jesus. In Matthew's version, he asks:

"What good thing must I do to get eternal life?"

This is a common trap we easily fall into. It is the fallen human nature. We want to make our salvation about ourselves.

We may not realize it, but most of us believe we can reform ourselves into the sort of people who will be pleasing to God.

So Jesus tells the young man he must keep the commandments.

Jesus is being ironic, telling him exactly what the Pharisees would say. The young man is clearly prepared for this question when he says, "All these I have kept...what do I still lack?"

The young man presumably understands the Judaic law and has reformed his behavior in accordance with it. However, his heart is still restless. He knows he is still lacking something.

Our heart's greatest desire is for God, but we will try to fill our hearts with our own efforts instead. The strongest among us will undergo personal reformation projects in which we will replace bad habits and destructive behavior with better habits and constructive behavior.

There is, of course, value in this. God wants us to grow, but we generally expect these efforts to fill our hearts, and we become discouraged when we are still lacking.

Jesus' gift to us is much more radical than reformation… Jesus offers transformation.

Paul tells us in Romans 12:2:

"Do not conform any longer to the pattern of this world, but be transformed by the renewing of your mind."

Although we can reform ourselves to a degree, it is not the solution we are looking for. Only God, through Jesus, can transform us, making us into the people we are meant to be.

<u>50</u>
Outward Deeds and the Inward Heart

Good morning kids! In the incident with the rich young ruler, the young man tells Jesus he has kept all of the commandments from his youth. He then asks, "What do I still lack?"

Jesus was teaching this man (and His disciples, who were standing by watching) about the difference between our outward deeds and our inward hearts. Just as with many of us, this young man had focused on how his life looked from the outside without considering what was in his own heart.

Jesus exposed this when He told him:

"One thing you lack…Go sell everything you have and give to the poor, and then you will have treasure in heaven. Then come follow me."

It says the young man went away discouraged because he had great wealth. The young man had attached his heart, and also his hope, to the things he had, and in his ability to do the right things.

Jesus showed him the void he felt in his heart could not be filled by anything the young man could do or achieve, but only by God alone.

Paul said in Romans 3:20:

"Therefore no one will be declared righteous in His sight by observing the law; rather, through the law we become conscious of sin."

When people place their trust in their own abilities to do all of the right things, eventually they will come to the realization of the rich young ruler. They will find that no amount of outward goodness can fix the sin in their hearts.

Jesus had made this clear in the Sermon on the Mount when He said if a person was angry or lustful, their heart was the same as that of a murderer or adulterer. So, something else must make people righteous, because no person is able to keep the whole spirit of the law in their hearts.

I think the dragon, Smaug, in JRR Tolkien's "The Hobbit," is a good image of this spirit.

Outwardly, the rich young ruler looked perfect, but when he was forced to look into his heart, he saw a dark cavern with a wretched and powerful dragon sitting upon the treasures of his heart.

He went away sad because he wasn't yet willing to let Jesus transform this hidden cavern into a place suitable for the Holy Spirit to dwell in.

51

He Looks at us and He Loves us

Good morning kids! The gospel writer, Mark, included a beautiful detail in his recounting of the rich young ruler. He said in Mark 10:21:

"Jesus looked at him and loved him."

The young man had faithfully lived a moral and productive life, and hoped Jesus could reveal to him another deed he could do to make himself finally happy.

He even believed he had perfectly kept all of the commandments. But unlike so many of the Pharisees, the young man was earnest.

I think Jesus looked at him and loved him because He knew the man felt the emptiness in his heart that could only be filled by the free gift of God.

I suspect it breaks Jesus' heart when He sees us striving to earn His approval, knowing all we really need to do is surrender our pride and sense of self-sufficiency. It is in this surrender that we become able to allow His love to flow into the place inside of us which is made to hold Him alone.

I feel like this young man so often. I feel like I'm trying so hard, yet I'm not making the progress I want to make. I sit down to quiet my heart and mind in order to offer up eloquent prayers, and I can hardly put together a single coherent sentence.

But looking at the rich young ruler, I am realizing this is a blessing. It is a spacious place I am unable to fill on my own. It is meant to be filled with God's grace. I just need to let go of my attachments; of my expectations about how I can fill myself up. I just need to wait patiently and hopefully for the Lord.

I am going to start using this verse as a prayer, except I am modifying it to say, "Jesus, you look at me and you love me." That is all.

I'm not going to worry about long and elaborate prayers that I can't focus on. I am going to try to pray this little prayer without ceasing, to whisper in my soul when I am anxious or restless, happy or sad, hopeful or downcast.

Jesus, you see me, and you love me. That is enough. It is the only thing I lack.

52
Dragon Skins

Good morning kids! When the rich young ruler came to see Jesus, he expected to be told a secret formula by which he could secure his own personal happiness by his own efforts. But with a single question Jesus cut through this surface level perspective of life. He cut the young man right to his heart, showing him he needed to desire God alone, more than his personal prosperity.

The young man went away so downcast, I think, because he had never realized, or even vaguely considered, that he had attached his heart so completely to his wealth and comfort.

I think he was crushed to discover his heart was deceitful; that it had so subtly misled him to believe he held the key to his own happiness; that if he did the right things, he would achieve success, favor and wealth, and contentment would naturally follow.

Like so many of us, he had unwittingly staked his happiness on the belief that his prosperity would be his reward; that it would provide the wholeness he longed for.

The rich young ruler reminds me of Eustice in CS Lewis's "The Voyage of the Dawn Treader." You'll recall Eustice discovers a hidden treasure in a cave where a dragon has died. He believes these riches will solve all of his problems, so he begins to gather up the treasure.

After having a nap, he discovers another dragon has come to the treasure. As he searches around, he is horrified to discover he has actually become that dragon. He tries to scrape the dragon skin off of himself, but he can't, just as no amount of good works had solved the rich young ruler's unhappiness.

It is only after he despairs of ever being able to save himself that he meets Aslan, who tells him He will have to remove the skin for him. We are told, "The very first tear he made was so deep that (Eustice) thought it had gone right into (his) heart. And when he began pulling the skin off, it hurt worse than anything (he'd) ever felt."

When Aslan had finished removing the scales, however, Eustice had been transformed back into a boy. But he was a new boy with a transformed understanding of life.

And here is what I imagine about the after-story of the rich young ruler.

I believe the young man had an authentic encounter with Jesus, and went away so downcast because Jesus had made just such a cut into his own dragon scales. It was the first cut into the wholeness the young man was seeking.

It can be a little scary and discouraging when we meet Jesus and He starts to transform us. It is hard to believe He will really be better than the things we have trusted in. But He is patient to hold our hands as we learn to detach our hearts from these lies and follow after Him as He makes us new.

53
Trusting in Our Riches

Good morning kids! This text is a little longer because it's about a passage I find a bit confusing.

After the rich young ruler had left, Jesus tells His disciples it is harder for a rich person to enter the kingdom of heaven than for a camel to fit through the eye of a needle.

This passage has always troubled me because I'm not sure at what point someone is considered rich. I am not sure how to tell when people become rich enough to jeopardize their ability to enter the kingdom of heaven.

Relative to the world's population, the vast majority of North Americans might be considered rich. So, is Jesus saying it is unlikely any of us can enter into God's kingdom?

Or is He just referring to the people who are extremely rich – much richer than us? But again, this implies there is some arbitrary point at which a person goes from not being rich to being rich.

So, I have been looking at this passage in Mark more closely to see what the original Greek said. I've also been reading a variety of commentators for their interpretations. What I'm finding is it seems as if most of our translations misinterpret it.

Mark 10:23 did not originally say "how hard it is for the rich," but rather, "how hard it is for those who have riches." And then in verse 24, it literally says, "those who trust in their riches."

Jesus is not making an arbitrary distinction between people who are rich and people who are not rich by the world's estimation. As always, Jesus is looking at what is in a person's heart.

I think Jesus is talking to virtually everyone in our modern world. We are all trained from our youth to trust in our riches, in the things we have. Even the poorest people among us generally follow this mindset of trusting in our riches, because even when we don't have much, we still tend to tie our hopes to getting more.

And if we have lost hope in life because we can't seem to get ahead, this shows definitively that we are trusting in our riches, because we don't believe we can be content without them.

I am guilty of this. Even when it is not a conscious thought, the deception in my heart, based upon the world's ideas, has become so thoroughly entrenched in my soul that I am not even aware of it.

If I'm honest, I really do believe I would be happier if I had just a little more; that I would be more content if I could afford slightly nicer things. I would be less anxious if I could pay off a bit more of my debt, or if I could get more money into savings.

I really would be more content and less anxious for a time, which is Jesus' point, because it would be based upon what I have and do. It would not be based upon the goodness of God.

Jesus is not saying it is bad to have money. He encourages us to be prudent and generous with the money He has blessed us with. But He is saying we should not trust in our riches, because these hopes are training us to ignore the true nature of our own hearts.

Even the disciples, who are with Jesus, assume salvation, the filling of our hearts, is partly contingent on what we have, asking in Mark 10:26, "who then can be saved?"

And this is where Jesus shifts the focus away from riches to all of humanity.

He says in Mark 10:27, "With people this is impossible, but not with God; all things are possible with God." Jesus confirms people cannot save themselves. People cannot fill their own hearts. People cannot be saved by their own efforts.

The disciples don't understand that Jesus is telling them, yet again, He Himself IS the possibility of God. He is able to do what we cannot. It is only by placing our trust in Jesus that we can enter into God's kingdom. Only Jesus can fill our hearts with the unshakable hope of salvation; all of us, the rich and the poor alike.

<u>54</u>
Being Still

Good morning kids! I was thinking about how we can live a contemplative life in the modern world. The Psalmist said in 46:10:

"Be still and know that I am God."

It is difficult to be still in our lives. But I was thinking part of being still is just being available – being open to God's presence in our lives even as we are moving about in them – that this is a part of living a contemplative life.

As I was thinking, a memory came to me which I have always considered a holy moment in my life.

At the very beginning of my freshman year of college, I was going to different campus ministries trying to meet people, hoping to find some like-minded friends. This time was exciting, but also a little scary and a little lonely.

After one of these meetings, I followed a group of people who were going to drive up Big Thompson Canyon below Estes Park to build a campfire and sing praise music. After driving for about an hour up into the mountains, we found a good spot along the river to build a fire, so we parked near the road.

Everyone walked down a trail, about 50 yards long, away from our cars to the river side. On either side of the trail was thick and tall mountain grass.

As everyone was talking and singing, I was feeling awkward. After a time, I began to slowly back out of the firelight into the darkness, so I could leave unnoticed.

As I walked back to my car I looked up at the stars. The night was still and moonless and dark between the remote canyon walls.

So, I pulled my sleeping bag from my car and quietly laid down in the tall mountain grass a dozen yards off the path. I laid still and felt like the splendor of the heavens were washing over me.

Every so often, a meteor would burn up in the atmosphere, sending a brief streak through the periphery of my vision. God was moving and present.

Gradually the group began to depart until one last person put out the fire. And then I was alone, lying down in the grass, in the pitch darkness, in silent awe.

I was truly contemplative; just open and available to the wonder of God.

Time slipped by – perhaps a couple of hours – well past midnight – and I continued to stare contentedly into the sky when an especially large meteor burned across the night from one horizon clear across to the other horizon emblazoning a sharp streak across the darkness.

I unconsciously spoke into the darkness, "WHOOOAAA."

And perhaps thirty feet away, another voice, as if a perfectly timed echo also gasped, "WHOOOAAA." After the initial fright, this stranger and I laughed, realizing we were unknowingly sharing in this display of God's transcendence.

We didn't talk much. It felt like a grand finale, so we quietly collected our sleeping bags and headed back home.

He did become one of my first college friends. Three years later he even stood at my wedding as one of my groomsmen.

I don't have much of a point except to say, when we make ourselves available to God, He shows up with things we need. It doesn't necessarily require hours of stillness in the night. We just need to practice being open to Him as often as we are able, even in the moment-to-moment-ness of our regular lives. He will show up now and then, reminding us of His love, and that we are not alone.

<u>55</u>
Abundant Life

Good morning kids! I have been thinking this week about John 10:10 where Jesus says:

"The thief comes only to steal and kill and destroy; I came so that they would have life, and have it abundantly."

I feel so vulnerable to the thief's disruption of my heart and my mind.

This is another place where I think we make the promises of Jesus about our efforts and we suffer badly as a result. We imagine the abundant life of Jesus is a journey; that it is a place we are working towards while we deal with the constant destruction of the thief meddling in our lives.

Some people think the abundant life we are working towards is heaven, but I think this reading misses the intended message. While Jesus does promise eternal life, He also came that we might have a meaningful life now; that we might have promise and power, hope and peace – all amidst the peril and threats around us this very day.

He did not come just to give us abundant life to journey towards. He came that we might have abundant life for the journey.

The word "abundance" implies having the full amount of something, beyond the expected limit, continually all around us. When we accept Jesus into our lives, the Holy Spirit takes up residence within our hearts, and He brings the abundant life of Christ with Him.

But we are still fallen people who cling so easily to lies and despair. It is difficult to make ourselves available to the abundant life of Jesus. We are so accustomed to going through the motions of life that it becomes increasingly difficult to really live it, to enjoy it abundantly.

The world teaches us to focus on the tasks of life, to concentrate so we can achieve. I am not saying it isn't sometimes necessary to focus. When I am flying in a plane, I hope my pilot is focused. But I also hope she is not so focused that she is closed off to the sounds of the engines, to the look of the surrounding sky, to the readings of the various gauges.

The abundant life of Jesus is more about making ourselves open and available to His Spirit than it is about concentrating on one thing at a time, over and over, so that we miss what is happening around us and within us.

Jesus calls us to an abundant life, in all of its monotony, as well as its momentousness. If we will only pay attention, He continually offers us the fullness of His presence while we go from task to task; even while we clean the house or do the dishes.

56
Don't Worry

Good morning kids! Jesus famously told us not to worry during His Sermon on the Mount, recorded in Matthew 6:25-34.

One of the things that blocks us from experiencing the fullness of Christ is worry. I, personally, am very prone to worry. But Jesus wants us to trust He will take care of us. He says to consider the birds of the air and the lilies of the field.

God provides for the birds even though they do not sow or reap, or labor or spin. The birds of the air enjoy their flight in the present moment, riding the wind that is in the sky now.

The lilies of the field are beautiful in their season as they reflect God's glory. They do not worry that they will soon wither and fade through the upcoming winter.

Jesus tells us we are far more valuable than these birds and flowers He has provided for, and yet we have such little faith. We foolishly think we can enhance our lives by worrying.

I don't think Jesus is saying to never think about tomorrow, or to not make plans for tomorrow. But He always wants us to return to the present moment. He doesn't want us to fixate on the future with worry.

The word He used for worry means to be divided; to be split apart; to be distracted. When we are divided, we are trying to be in two places at once. Jesus wants us to be whole, to be present in the one place where we are right now.

He tells us to seek first God and His righteousness, and trust He will take care of us. He means for us to seek Him first, over and over throughout each day, until it is a habit.

God's plan for us to experience the abundant life of Jesus is fairly simple, but we are divided. We are always rushing to the next thing, so we are not present in the current thing.

Or we are caught dwelling so much on previous things that we are oblivious to the new things God has brought us today.

We are preoccupied with taking care of ourselves. We are constantly thinking, Jesus said, "What shall we eat? What shall we drink? What shall we wear?" We distract our souls from the wholeness of God that He intends to fill our lives with in every moment, as they are happening.

God is with us in each moment if we will make ourselves available to Him. We do not have to worry, because He wants to meet us in the present moment. He wants to meet us in our work and in our play, in our relationships and in our aloneness. He wants to meet us in this very moment, even as we go about living the lives He has given us today.

57
Spiritual Adoption

Good morning kids! God is always giving us glimpses into His character, if our eyes and ears are open to see and hear it. For me, M and R's intention to adopt J has given me one of these opportunities.

Normally, when we think of adoption, we think of people adopting babies or toddlers, so these children will grow up as beloved members of a family. They will not know the loneliness of being orphans, nor will they experience the uncertainty of moving between various foster homes. They won't remember not being part of a family.

In M and R's case, they are adopting an 18-year-old. They are adopting a legal adult. I didn't even realize this was something that could be done before they told me.

It makes me think of how Paul uses the metaphor of adoption in several of his letters. I think the idea of being adopted as an adult, or as someone who has been an orphan and longs for a family, shines a greater light on Paul's example. The following passage is from Galatians 4:4-7. Where you see "orphan," Paul actually said "slave." I felt this switch would help you see the idea more easily:

"But when the right time came, God sent his Son, born of a woman, subject to the law. God sent Him to buy freedom for us who were (orphans), so that he could *adopt* us as his very own children. And because we are his children, God has sent the Spirit of his Son into our hearts, prompting us to call out, 'Abba, Father.' Now you are no longer an (orphan) but God's own child. And since you are his child, God has made you his heir."

In Paul's example, we are not adopted as infants. We are adopted as grown people who have come to realize we are orphans in the world. Jesus did not merely come to show us the way to an independence that gives us an identity apart from being orphans. He came to make us children of God.

This is how it is with our longing for God; with our hope to have our hearts filled by His love. This is why God sent His Son. In His sacrifice, Paul says Jesus enabled us to be adopted as the actual children of God.

Because we are His children, He sends His Spirit into our hearts so we become full. We are no longer orphans. He gives us a home in this world; a place we can always come to for love and support.

We are not merely being mentored, learning from Christ. We have become the children of God. Our debts are canceled and we receive a new name. Jesus has enabled us to become the legal children of God, with all of the rights and benefits of being His children.

58
Talking to Ourselves

Good morning kids! I have been struggling through some despondency and writer's block over the past few weeks. Throughout this time, I have been parked at Psalms 42 and 43. The Psalmist repeats three times in verses 42:5, 11 and 43:5:

"Why are you in despair, my soul? And why are you restless within me? Wait for God, for I will again praise Him for the help of His presence, my God."

I think it is interesting he is troubled and restless, and he doesn't know why. This is how it is so often with me. In many ways I feel like I am living as well as I ever have done, and yet I am more prone than ever to despair and anxiety.

We all struggle with being ruled by our emotions. They often push us this way and pull us that way with no real rhyme or reason. And we let them.

Like the Psalmist, we need to talk to ourselves. Why is my soul in despair? Why is it restless?

As I have been reading these verses for the last few weeks, some of my struggle has been because part of me doesn't really want to talk to myself.

Part of me takes an unhealthy satisfaction in my melancholy and wants to sail aimlessly through this fog that sometimes rolls in over the ocean I'm floating upon; to drift along with my hand off the rudder.

We forget those times when God, in His love, gave us glimpses of the far distant land that made us climb into our boats and push out into the waters in the first place. We forget how time and again we have seen distant peaks breaking through the clouds, enabling us to aim ourselves towards God's promises for us.

But the Psalmist does not merely question his emotions, he goes on to tell himself to wait for God. He reminds himself to place his hope and trust in God.

He reminds himself, even though he doesn't see Him now, he will eventually praise God again for the help of His presence. This doesn't mean he can create happy emotions and change the feelings in his heart, but he can remind himself to steer towards the hope of God and His presence.

We will do this over and over throughout our lives. Although we are saved by Christ once and for all – although we climb down into our boats to sail to the place God has made for us just one time – our salvation is a lifelong journey over ever-changing seas.

We will continue to question our souls about why they are downcast and disturbed, because the Holy Spirit is teaching us to put our hope in God. And every time we do this, we journey further out into the waters towards the help and promise of the presence of God.

59
Doing Everything as if We're Doing it for God

Good morning kids! I have been thinking of the verses that talk about doing everything for God, such as Colossians 3:17:

"And whatever you do, whether in word or deed, do it all in the name of the Lord Jesus, giving thanks to God the Father through him."

It seems fairly straightforward, and when we hear people refer to this verse, they seem to suggest it is indeed quite simple.

But when I look up commentaries on this verse, virtually all writers say essentially, "do everything as if you're doing it for God... and here are the necessary steps to do everything for God."

The steps vary, but they all seem to be rooted in dependence upon our own ability to work our way to God.

While the idea may seem simple, this is one of those concepts I really struggle with. How can I do everything for God? All my work? All my deeds? All my thoughts and words? It makes me wonder if I'm the only person in Christendom with a constant battle raging in my soul between my selfish willfulness, and willingness to seek after Jesus with my whole heart.

I think we are easily tricked by our own hearts and minds. I have often determined I would do some specific thing to honor another person. I even imagined I was doing that thing in the name of Jesus.

But, if I'm honest, I most often do things with an expectation of recognition for the good things I've done. I expect particular rewards for my efforts. I expect God and others to give me certain things for my "selflessness."

The problem is, this constant spirit of expectation turns our focus to ourselves and away from God. If we do things with expectations about what we should get, we will be disappointed, because other people might not notice or appreciate our efforts.

They might even criticize our efforts. And they might be right, because sometimes we try hard to do something good, but it's not really the good thing we should actually be doing. It's just the good thing we think will get us what we want the fastest.

This sets us up for discouragement, because we are depending upon the efforts of our own perceived goodness to get us what we think we want – what we think we need – what we believe will make us happy.

From my experience, I often think I am trying to do things for God, but my disappointment with the results is a sure sign I'm actually doing it for myself.

But this is good news. God is getting me out of my own way. He is showing me the promise of working for Him; of experiencing His relationship in greater depth. He is saving me from missing real joy by running after counterfeit happiness that is actually based upon my own pride.

When we do things like we're doing them for God, it doesn't necessarily mean we will be more successful by the world's standards. It does mean, though, we will increasingly discover true contentment and joy, because God will be there. We will become more present before God, because we won't be preoccupied with what we're going to get for our efforts.

<u>60</u>
Justification and Sanctification

Good morning kids! I have been reading over several of Paul's letters and was noticing how he often talks about two things: how we were saved once and for all by having faith in Christ's sacrifice, and also about what that should mean for how we live our lives going forward. The biblical terms for these two ideas are justification and sanctification.

Justification releases us from the penalty of sin, and sanctification delivers us from the power of sin.

Paul often likens our lives apart from Christ to being held prisoners by our sinful natures. Justification is the pounding of the judge's gavel, declaring us innocent. By Christ's death and resurrection, we have been released from the prisons of our sin. We can leave. We are free to go. So, we step out into our permanent freedom, down the path into our new lives. We have been declared innocent once and for all, but now we have to make daily decisions as free people.

The problem is, although we have been justified by Christ, our hearts and minds still have a tendency towards the things that had us in prison to begin with. The path of least resistance is to accept the gift of Christ's salvation, and then continue to live the same way we always did; to continue to be led by our own self-interest, trying to please ourselves alone. This path is to accept the justification of God, and then continue to live as if we were still in prison.

Paul says in Galatians 5:1:

"It is for freedom that Christ has set us free. Stand firm, then, and do not let yourselves be burdened again by a yoke of slavery."

Christ does not simply free us from our guilt and then send us on our ways. When God releases us from prison, He sends the Holy Spirit to teach us to live as free people. We begin the lifelong journey of gradually being delivered from the power of sin, step-by-step. This is sanctification.

Justification and sanctification are both based on Christ's redeeming sacrifice, but the first is once for all time, and the second is in the moment-to-moment-ness of life being lived out. By sanctifying us, God is transforming us into people who can love Him and are able to enjoy His freedom.

He wants to redeem us each day through the regular living of our lives. He wants to meet us in the next decision we face this very day, so we might learn to experience life in unity with Him and the Holy Spirit. He is slowly purifying our intentions; giving us His heart; teaching us to desire Him more than the things that still draw us away against our best intentions. Sanctification teaches us to live each day of our lives in light of Christ's permanent justification which we received at the very beginning.

61
Rain That Often Falls

Good morning kids! These last several days I've been thinking about Hebrews 6:7:

"Land that drinks in the rain often falling on it and that produces a crop useful to those for whom it is farmed receives the blessing of God."

It is interesting to me that he says the rain often, or continually, falls on the land. In reality, though, Israel receives most of its moisture during rainy seasons. Over the course of a full year, there are long dry stretches where rain does not fall upon it, even in the most fertile areas.

I think the writer is comparing our lives to a field where a farmer plants a crop of vegetables from which they hope to feed themselves. He is suggesting our lives can continually have the blessing of God, so we can enjoy nourishment for our souls through all seasons.

This differs from much of our experience, though, where it is so easy to pass through our lives, just trying to get from one moment to the next; just trying to get through the work day, or the school day, so we can get home and hopefully relax for a few minutes before we go to bed and do it all over again.

It is so easy to surrender to the monotony, to be dominated by our calendars, just trying to get from one appointment to the next. Our souls can feel like barren fields without much of a crop to sustain us.

But if we are paying attention, God is continually providing rain to the soil of our souls. We have the opportunity to accept everything in our lives as the blessing of God. He continually provides rain which we can drink into our souls. All of our experiences, pleasant or uncomfortable or boring, are useful for cultivating the health of our spirits so we can produce a bountiful crop.

Rather than stumbling from one thing to another throughout our day, we need to pay attention to what is happening. We need to remember we are daughters and sons of God, and He is speaking to us in the details of our lives. He is causing rain to often fall upon the soil of our souls for us to drink it in. All of these moments can be useful for us. They are the blessing of God if we are patient enough to be present in them.

62
The Anchor of our Soul

Good morning kids! I think I've written before about the metaphors of ships and anchors, but I want to look at them again today. There is actually only one verse in the Bible that uses this analogy directly.

Hebrews 6:19 says:

"We have this hope as an anchor for the soul, firm and secure. It enters the inner sanctuary behind the curtain, where Jesus, who went before us, has entered on our behalf."

We are like ships sailing through the seas of our lives. When the seas are smooth and the winds calm, we don't think much about the anchor coiled up under the deck. During those times, we have a tendency to place our hopes in ourselves.

Hope is often a fluttering emotion inside our hearts reassuring us everything will work out the way we want it to…until it doesn't. When the winds pick up and clouds descend, when we start to lose sight of the harbor towards which we thought we were aiming, those fluttering hopes will fly away.

Those are the moments when we turn our gaze outside of ourselves. We wonder what we can possibly hope in… Friends? Family? Careers? These are all good things, but they are not ultimate things. They will also fail to meet our hopes at some point. This is especially discouraging, because they are good things.

The writer tells us there is only one hope we have as an anchor for our soul that is firm and secure.

Regarding anchors, I was recently reading about a battleship weighing 100,000 tons (or 200 million pounds). The anchor for this ship weighed 30,000 pounds, which is the equivalent of about 7 Toyota 4Runners.

And that is just the anchor. The anchor is of no use unless it is attached to the ship by a strong and reliable cable. In the case of this ship, each individual chain link in the cable weighed an additional 136 pounds.

Given the massive weight of this anchor, you can imagine when it is dropped, it will descend incredibly fast, quickly plunging out of sight into the darkness of the sea until it reaches the hidden solid ground of the ocean floor. And when it digs into the ground, it is strong enough to steady the weight of the ship. It is held firm by the strength of the chain. It will not break.

The writer tells us Jesus is our hope, the anchor of our souls. We attach our hope to Him like the anchor cable. And just as the anchor passes through the mysterious darkness of the ocean, it says Jesus has passed through the inner sanctuary behind the curtain into the holy of holies, into the very presence of God.

He is our anchor that passes through unseen mysteries until He attaches us to the very throne of God. We cannot see the throne, and we cannot see the mysteries the anchor chain passes through, but we can trust in its strength to hold us firm and secure.

63
Being a Christian

Good morning kids! I want to talk a little bit about what it means when we consider whether or not to call ourselves "Christians." It can be confusing, because most of us have objections to some things other Christians say we have to believe in order to be Christians.

These people can be very persuasive by quoting Bible verses to support their views regarding these issues they think are essential to our faith. Unfortunately, this can be mistaken for telling would-be believers, "That's great you think you might want to follow Jesus, but if you really want to be a Christian, you need to believe these other things too."

Many people walk away at this point because they decide they can't believe everything these Christians say they have to believe. The problem is this assumes all of our objections have to be satisfied before we'll consider Christ.

Christians sometimes encourage this error by focusing faith on controversies. They are essentially trying to establish a set of codes people have to acknowledge in order to be Christians.

This attitude is what Jesus regularly criticized the Pharisees for.

My desire for you kids is God would protect you from these distractions. They are chasing people away when they are on the very cusp of encountering Jesus.

I want you to know that being a Christian ultimately boils down to what we think about the resurrection of Christ.

Paul says in 1 Corinthians 15:14:

"And if Christ has not been raised, then all our preaching is useless, and your faith is useless."

In other words, if Jesus was not raised, your objections don't matter and there would be no such thing as authentic Christianity. It would just be a name for another arbitrary self-help club.

Christianity starts by looking at Jesus' life, death and resurrection as it is shown in the gospels. A Christian is a person who believes Jesus lived, died and was resurrected, and their life is forever changed by that fact.

When you become a Christian, you become someone whose life is transformed by a central desire to know the risen Christ personally for the remainder of your life. It is not a desire to know a set of rules, but to know Him.

Having objections and disagreeing with other Christians about various issues is not bad. But these issues should not be road blocks keeping us away from Jesus.

Rather, they are things people with hearts being transformed by the love and power of Christ will begin to work out in their personal relationships with God. They are questions Jesus wants to help us answer along the way, as we walk our own unique path with Him throughout our lives. They do not define us, and they should never be mistaken for our basic faith in Jesus.

The answers to those objections won't change a person's heart. Those things are focused on a person's mind, not their hearts.

Jesus is the key to our faith as Christians, and it is only in His resurrection that our hearts can be opened to His transforming Spirit. And Jesus does not withhold His Spirit from anyone who truly desires Him, regardless of their opinions.

64
Clothing Yourselves with Christ

Good morning kids! Many people in our society are preoccupied with creating an image of who they are in order to present it over social media. Society's message is that what we think of ourselves is the truest and most important thing about ourselves.

This trains us to think of every belief and idea, not in terms of truth, but instead, according to whether we think it fits us.

We are encouraged to accept every idea of truth as if it were an outfit to try on. We are told we have to accept every idea as equally true until we try it on ourselves. Just as with clothes, people will say, "That looks good on you, but it doesn't fit me."

The problem is, what fits us will change over the course of our lives. What fits today will wear out and look out of style tomorrow, so we'll have to figure out what fits us then.

The irony is, this way we think of ourselves is at the root of why we feel so uncertain to begin with, because the way we identify ourselves is so often a denial of the person God actually created us to be.

Paul said in Romans 13:14:

"Rather, clothe yourselves with the Lord Jesus Christ."

To be followers of Christ reverses the belief about our personal identity. We don't begin by asking if Christ fits who we are because Christianity doesn't start with us. It is not about trying to fashion a belief system that reinforces whatever our ideas are about ourselves today.

Our identity is based upon a personal God who created us uniquely to be in a relationship with Him. Jesus fits all of us uniquely. To be a Christian is to believe our identity is in Christ; that we are able to put Him on, and He will always fit.

Paul says in Colossians 3:9-10, when we take off our old selves and put on our new selves, we will begin to be renewed in the image of God, because we are putting on Christ.

Putting on Christ is the only outfit that changes us from the inside out, and this outfit will only look better and better as it gets older.

65
Not Just all People, but Each Person

Good morning kids! As I have been considering the idea of what it means to call ourselves Christians, I have been scanning through Paul's letters because he spends a great deal of time expounding on the wonder of what Christ has done, and how He is at the core of our faith.

Today I want to look at just the second half of Galatians 2:20, where Paul said:

"The life I now live in the body, I live by faith in the Son of God, who loved me and gave himself for me."

I think it is interesting he did not say Jesus loved all people and died for all people. Instead, he said Jesus loved him personally, and died for him personally. We tend to read over this too quickly.

Our minds generalize the meaning, vaguely recognizing Jesus died for everyone. But when Paul said He died "for him," he was also saying Christ died "instead of him." Paul recognized he deserved the death Christ bore because of the way he had personally rejected God throughout his life, but that Christ took his place anyhow.

Paul made the substitutionary death of Christ personal, not general.

People have a tendency to move into generalizations because it allows them to focus outside of themselves, at "them" instead of "me." Without realizing it, we can easily become comfortable in our faith and slide into focusing on how Christ died for all of them – a vague mass of unknown people.

We might also lump ourselves into the general mass of people by saying Christ died for all of us. This depersonalizes our own selves by vaguely including us in the impersonal mass of everyone.

It is more accurate to say He died for each of them – each of us – each unique and beloved human being.

Christ is personal. One of the things that makes Christianity unique is Christ breaks the vague mass of all people into parts, so rather than just giving Himself for all people, He more specifically gave Himself for each individual person, even me. He loved me and gave Himself for me.

<u>66</u>
The Marine Layer

Good morning kids! I was recently thinking about summers in San Diego during the few years I lived there during high school.

When people think of summer at the beach, they think of clear sunshiny days. But beginning in May, and lasting through most of the month of June, pretty much every day starts off with dark and foggy overcast skies.

This is called the Marine Layer. This happens because the water flowing down along the coastline from the north is notably cooler at this time of year relative to the water further offshore, which creates clouds each night.

Meanwhile, the inland desert is really starting to heat up. This difference in cool temperatures at the beach and hot temperatures in the desert creates the familiar breeze that blows from the ocean towards the land.

Because of these differences, the clouds forming offshore every night are blown in over the coastline, so each morning starts in a damp cloudy haze.

But these clouds are not like the clouds we are used to in Colorado, that are high up in the atmosphere. These clouds are damper, compressed between the beach and inland mountains. At most, they are only a few thousand feet high.

So, not far overhead, the summer sun is slowly rising into unseen clear blue skies. As it quietly rises, it gradually burns off the marine layer. On most days, it totally evaporates by lunch time, giving way to bright sunshine.

The prophet, Isaiah, says in verse 18:4:

"I will remain quiet and will look on from my dwelling place, like shimmering heat in the sunshine."

Sin, and the discouragement we experience when we place our hopes in the things of the world, rather than in God, is like an overcast sky darkening our lives.

It rolls in thick over our hearts and we can't see more than a few feet in front of ourselves. It can cause us to feel like we're walking around in a fog.

But we are children of God. He is there, quietly looking upon us. His love and mercy are always shimmering down upon the fog we are walking around in. He is teaching us to trust that His grace is shining above the clouds, slowly evaporating our sin and despondency.

When we learn to be patient, to focus on the hope of the sunshine blazing just above our sin and fear and anxiety, the mist we are walking in will eventually melt into blue. By the heat of His love alone, we will find we are no longer surrounded by fog, but are instead bathing in the warmth of God's goodness.

<u>67</u>
Life By Comparison

Good morning kids! The verses for my text today are from the end of the gospel of John. Jesus is talking to Peter and asks him three times if Peter loves him, matching the three times Peter had denied Jesus before He was crucified.

In the end, Jesus foreshadows how Peter would eventually die, and then simply commands Peter to follow Him. Peter then turns, looks at John, and asks Jesus, "Lord, what about him?" Jesus responds in verse 21:22:

"What is that to you? You must follow me."

Throughout our lives we compare ourselves to one another. It is one of the primary ways we define who we are.

The grades we receive throughout school, although they show how well we have learned various subjects, ultimately take on meaning in comparison to other students.

We receive performance reviews at work to compare which employees do job tasks more efficiently or profitably.

Advertising is also based on comparison, because it establishes an ideal for us to compare ourselves to. It is selling us ways to look better, feel better, perform better, achieve more. It attempts to place an image of success or happiness in our minds, and then it tries to suggest that our lives fall a bit short in comparison.

Social media is perhaps the most subtle and destructive platform for comparison. We all flip through our apps and unconsciously train our minds to compare ourselves to each post we see. Whether we realize it or not, we are unconsciously telling ourselves over and over, "she's prettier than me," "I wish I could be as tall and muscular as him," "they're happier than me because they go on better vacations," "I can't believe that person thinks they're cool," and it goes on and on.

We are so trained to monitor our progress in life by comparison, it is only natural we would also monitor our faith the same way. Even Peter, listening to the resurrected Jesus speak of his personal future, immediately turns his attention to John. He wants to know what John's future holds. It is as if he must see how his relationship with Jesus compares to John's relationship with Jesus for it to be meaningful.

Our sinful natures encourage us to become discouraged by how we are less faithful, or less joyful, or less intelligent, or less spiritual than other people.

They also encourage us to become prideful, so we base our confidence upon the ways we may think we are better than other people. We may allow ourselves to humbly admit we're not perfect, but then we take reassurance in the ways we think we are better, or more moral, or more faithful than some other people.

But Jesus says to Peter, "Whatever I do with John is none of your business. I only require that you follow me."

This is great news, because it means Jesus sends His Holy Spirit into each of us individually, so He can lead us each down our own paths. He wants to free us from the bondage of comparison.

Of course, we will encourage one another, and we will meet together in our communities of believers, but this is to spur one another on along our journeys as each person follows Jesus. It is not to perform and compare. It is the same Jesus we each follow, but your path is your own to share with Jesus in your unique way.

Jesus is not going to look at you as being inferior to one person, or superior to another person. He is not comparing you to anyone else. He is simply looking at you and at your willingness to follow Him in your own places.

68
Making Us Acceptable

Good morning kids! One of my greatest struggles in following Jesus is I continually take my eyes off of Him and try to earn His approval by my performance. I try to discipline myself to be a good person. This is the way of the world, and it is so deeply ingrained in our minds that it takes a lifetime of following Jesus to unlearn it.

We think if we do well, if we discipline ourselves, we will be accepted. We will be accepted at school. We will be accepted at work. We will be accepted by our families. We will be accepted by our friends.

So, why wouldn't it be the same with God? It feels so natural to believe if I do well, if I discipline myself to be a good person, this is how I will be accepted by God. This is the world's perception of religion. Our goodness is about us and our efforts.

This is where Christianity differs from other world-views. Paul says in Galatians 3:2-3:

"Let me ask you this one question: Did you receive the Holy Spirit by obeying the law of Moses? Of course not! You received the Spirit because you believed the message you heard about Christ. How foolish can you be? After starting your new lives in the Spirit, why are you now trying to become perfect by your own human effort?"

Paul says we become Christians when we believe the message of Christ, which means we come to a point where we recognize we cannot make ourselves acceptable to God through our goodness or obedience.

So, we lay aside our old lives. We come to believe Christ's perfection, and sacrifice in our place, has made us perfect and acceptable to God. The only part we have played in this is simply to believe. By believing, we have received new life through the Holy Spirit which helps us to participate in the perfection of Christ.

But this is where we all tend to revert back to the world's thinking. As Paul says, after we start our new lives in the Spirit, we go on trying to make ourselves perfect by our own human effort again.

We treat Jesus as if He merely lent us a hand in a tough spot; as if He pulled us up over a difficult ledge on the mountain we're climbing. Now that we're through that tight spot, we like to think we can handle the rest on our own. Jesus is just our fallback strategy.

It is in our natures to want our goodness to be about ourselves. We want to be God. We want to make ourselves acceptable by our own efforts. We want to prove we can climb that mountain without any help. We want to take credit for our righteousness.

Or, sometimes we might go to the opposite extreme. We might use Jesus as an excuse to not try at all. We can make the mistake of not caring about our goodness, because we think if we were made perfect by Jesus alone, why does it matter if we do the right thing or not? If He's forgiven us once and for all, who cares what we do now?

In the end, I think we should very much care what we do now. When we begin to live our new lives in the Spirit, we should try to do the right things, but the reason why we try changes. During this journey of following Jesus, we slowly learn to make our goodness about Jesus, rather than about our own efforts to be good apart from Jesus.

In one of Timothy Keller's sermons, he summarized this idea in a way that I find really helpful: "The world says I obey therefore I am accepted. The gospel says I'm accepted therefore I obey."

This is what I am slowly learning over the last 40 years. By the grace of Christ alone, I am little-by-little learning to obey God simply out of gratitude for His unconditional love and acceptance of me, with less consideration of how hard I am trying.

<u>69</u>
The God Who Bears Our Burdens

Good morning kids! I have a tendency to feel burdened by a great many things in my life. As I get older, I justify this tendency by convincing myself these burdens are very important. They are not the petty burdens I carried when I was younger. I believe these burdens must be taken more seriously, as if it would be irresponsible not to be burdened so.

I have recently been saying to Mom that it feels overwhelming, how every day seems to brings so many difficult and complicated situations, and it feels unsustainable. I just want to sleep and get a reprieve from the pressure.

I feel burdened by the pace and cost of our lives. I feel burdened by growing my business at a rate that can keep pace. But even more than this, I feel burdened by providing spiritually and emotionally for all of you kids.

Whenever you are upset or discouraged, I feel like I need to somehow take your burdens away. Whether you give them to me or not, I try to take your burdens on top of my own anyhow.

As if this weren't enough, I am further burdened by my own sin – by a persistent whisper that I am not sufficient – that I'm not strong enough.

The Psalmist says in 68:19:

"Praise be to the Lord, to God our Savior, who daily bears our burdens."

I have often said we are each journeying along a unique path day-by-day. It is so easy to forget, though, that God is journeying with us. He is there daily.

I am carrying this tremendous pack, and at every stop I add more weight, so I feel like I can hardly stand up. Yet, there is God, walking silently beside me, offering to bear my burdens, offering to carry my pack for me. It takes a humility I have yet to achieve to set my pack down and offer my load to God.

But I am convinced God continues to travel along with us nonetheless. I am also hopeful we will eventually recognize His true character. We will have days where we find the humility to let Him carry our burdens, if only for a few steps at a time.

When we experience the lightness of walking without our packs, it will cause praise and gratitude to grow in our spirits. When we allow God to bear our burdens, He will replace our self-absorbed anxiety and discouragement with His grace and hope, which will enable us to truly engage authentically in our lives.

70
Carrying Our Idols

Good morning kids! Yesterday, when I was talking about burdens, I came across an interesting passage in Isaiah. In Isaiah 46:1-4, the writer is prophesying the fall of Babylon, which eventually occurred at the hands of Cyrus.

The Babylonians worshipped golden statues of their gods, so when they were conquered by Cyrus, Isaiah saw their gods being carried off into captivity along with the people. In verse 46:1 it says:

"Their idols are borne by beasts of burden. The images that are carried about are burdensome, a burden for the weary."

The idols of Babylon could not help the Babylonians. Not only were they unable to relieve the Babylonians of their burdens, the idols were, themselves, a tremendous burden. They were an overwhelming weight to be carried along by the people, even with the help of animals to share the load.

This is still the same today. We have idols we place our hopes in. We hope to be delivered by success, or affluence, or acceptance. But when we place our ultimate hope in these things – when we worship these things – they prove to be burdens. They are heavy golden statues that are a burden for weary people who must carry them into our captivity.

Isaiah goes on to contrast the idols of Babylon with God. God says, in Isaiah 46:3-4:

"I have upheld you since you were conceived, and have carried since your birth. Even to your old age and gray hairs I am He, I am He who will sustain you. I have made you and I will carry you."

God is not an impersonal statue. He has made us. We rarely realize it, but God carries us from the time we are born until we grow old. He intends to be our full hope who will sustain us for all of our days.

But God will not carry us when we are also trying to carry heavy idols towards a land of captivity. He wants us to let those things go, to set them down, to let them fall over like lifeless statues, so He can carry us out of captivity into a land of freedom.

71
Sharing His Yoke

Good morning kids! I am still thinking about how God wants me to understand burdens in my life. In the Psalms we looked at how God offers to bear our burdens. There are times when we take off our packs and lay them before Him, and He carries the entire load.

Then we looked at Isaiah where idols are burdens. We have a tendency to worship and place our hope in things besides God. These are idols we carry. They cannot deliver us from our weariness; rather, they make us weary from their weight. This is contrasted to God, who is a living God who not only offers to carry our loads, but He says He carries us throughout our lives like parents carry their children in their arms.

There is one other passage about burdens I want to consider. Jesus famously said in Matthew 11:28-30:

"Come to me, all you who are weary and burdened, and I will give you rest. Take my yoke upon you and learn from me, for I am gentle and humble in heart, and you will find rest for your souls. For my yoke is easy and my burden is light."

A yoke is a harness placed over the necks of animals such as oxen. It aligns the animals and distributes the weight of their load between them, enabling them to do more together than they could alone.

Jesus implies that, apart from God, we are made to bear our burdens individually. The burden I think we all bear, specifically, is to try and make ourselves perfect. We try to follow the law of morality and good conduct by our own power and goodness alone. This is a horrible burden, because all of the weight is on our own necks.

Jesus does not say we won't ever have burdens. He does not release us from the responsibility of growing in our character. What He does do is this: Jesus offers to come along beside us, to align Himself with us, placing a yoke over His back and ours so we might pull the plough more easily.

The really good news is Jesus has already ploughed this field on His own. He has borne the full weight, turning over the soil of this field that was once full of rocks and dead crops. By following the law of godliness perfectly, He has prepared the soil and, when we share His yoke, He will help us to bring forth a plentiful crop.

72
Where is Jesus' Tomb?

Good morning kids! In John 20:2 it says:

"So she came running to Simon Peter and the other disciple, the one Jesus loved, and said, 'They have taken the Lord out of the tomb, and we don't know where they have put Him!'"

I was thinking it is interesting we don't know exactly where the tomb of Jesus is located. There are a few ideas and traditions that speculate about where it might have been, but they are not certain.

If, however, for instance, you would like to visit the burial place of Mohammed, there is a great deal of certainty about where he was buried. Almost immediately upon his death, shrines were erected and his followers have been visiting them down to this very day.

So, I find it interesting that Jesus, who we know existed from multiple historical sources, even outside of the Christian tradition, does not have a certain burial site.

Even if His body was stolen and never found, as Mary feared, the early followers and disciples of Christ would have established a shrine at the tomb where He was initially buried. They would have continually visited that place to honor His memory and the principles He taught.

But they did not do that. They made no real effort to mark

the location of the tomb, because we are told by multiple gospel writers that He appeared to them alive, risen from the tomb.

The gospel writer, John, even emphasizes at the end of His book, "This is the disciple who testifies to these things and who wrote them down. We know that his testimony is true."

I suspect, as the Christian movement began to grow immediately after the resurrection of Christ, there were doubts about the initial gospels, and so John, as the only disciple who was not martyred, felt compelled to write an additional account of the life, death and resurrection of Jesus, to reiterate the fact that the body of Jesus was not at rest in a tomb, but rather to testify His body rose, and continued to live.

Jesus was the most influential religious figure in the history of the world, and yet there is no shrine built upon His final resting place, because He did not stay at rest.

Multiple witnesses bore testimony that He did not remain in the tomb. He rose from His tomb so He could give us true life. He continues to live and offer His Spirit to all of us who will accept it. We have the opportunity to experience the life of Christ within our own hearts so we too can testify to the reality of the living Christ.

<u>73</u>
The Weight That Slows Us Down

Good morning kids! In between other readings, I have also been very slowly reading through Hebrews this entire year. I have just come to Hebrews 12:1-2a where the writer says:

"Therefore, since we are surrounded by such a huge crowd of witnesses to the life of faith, let us strip off every weight that slows us down, especially the sin that so easily trips us up. And let us run with endurance the race God has set before us. Let us fix our eyes on Jesus."

This verse uses a couple of images I have already written about a few times: burdens and the life of faith as a race. What I never noticed before in this verse, regarding burdens, is the writer has two commands: He says to strip off the weight that slows us down, and especially strip off the sin that trips us up.

It is interesting he distinguishes between weight that slows us down, and weight that is sin which causes us to actually trip. I think the weight that slows us down could be legitimate things that aren't necessarily sins.

To run a fast race, it is important to minimize the weight we are carrying. I remember the first time I ran a mountain race, the 17-mile Imogene Pass Run, I carried a pack with two liters of water and enough food to last me an entire weekend. As I have learned how to race, I have stripped down on the amount of weight I carry so I can run faster for longer.

Our responsibilities, such as our family relationships, friendships and jobs, can become weights that slow us down in the life of faith. They are not sins. There are many Bible verses about how these are great gifts given to us by God. But if we carry them as burdens, we will not run the race of faith as well as we could. It would be like a runner carrying an excessively heavy backpack.

By stripping off these weights, we are not called to leave our families, friendships or jobs, but we are called to strip them off as burdens. It is a condition of the heart. As long as we are focused on those things as the most important things in our life, we cannot focus fully on Jesus.

The amazing thing is, when we release these good and legitimate things as burdens, and when we fix our eyes on Jesus, we know from other promises in the Bible that we grow to become more like Christ.

So, in the end, we will actually become better spouses, friends and workers than we ever could have been if we chose to make those things our ultimately important things. When our focus is Jesus, He redeems these important parts of our lives in a way we never could have on our own.

74
Faith is Not Stationary

Good morning kids! I want to look at yesterday's verse, Hebrews 12:1, again:

"Therefore, since we are surrounded by such a huge crowd of witnesses to the life of faith, let us strip off every weight that slows us down, especially the sin that so easily trips us up. And let us run with endurance the race God has set before us."

When we think about faith, we don't normally equate it with action. We are more likely to conjure images of people sitting quietly, meditating on God.

While this is indeed an important part of the life of faith, the writer here clearly has something more active in mind. He suggests God intends us to take up this faith we develop in stillness, and then to set out with a great effort. Truly living the life of faith requires the exertion of running a long race with endurance.

Faith is not merely stationary. Rather, we will find when we claim faith in the gift of Christ, God will immediately send us out to the starting line. He will ask us to set our eyes on Jesus and run the race towards the wonderful end He has set before us.

We are called to cast off our burdens; to step over the sins that trip us up; to run with endurance. This means it will often be uncomfortable. It will test our limits as we apply ourselves to the continuous persevering effort to run the course God has set before us.

But we will also find in the life of faith, it is Christ Himself who gives us the power to run.

I think many of us, though, don't embrace the effort the life of faith requires. We tend to think of the race as a moving walkway, like in airports, so the main effort required of us is to simply take that first step of faith, to step out onto the walkway.

From there we assume it will transport us to the end of the terminal where our departure gate is. In our wishful thinking, we imagine Jesus wants to do all of the work while we are comfortably transported along until we arrive at the end of our journey.

But God does not call us to step onto His moving walkway of faith. He calls us to engage our muscles, to stride forward and run with endurance. He calls us to apply our faith in seeking to know Him, to learn and grow. This effort to fix our eyes on Jesus will sometimes be difficult, but we will find, as we continue to run, it is Jesus Himself who gives us the very strength needed to live the life of faith; to run with endurance towards what God has set before us.

75
God's Discipline

Good morning kids! I want to look at Hebrews 12:10b-11 today:

"But God disciplines us for our good, that we may share in His holiness. No discipline seems pleasant at the time, but painful. Later on, however, it produces a harvest of righteousness and peace for those who have been trained by it."

I remember being moved by these verses when I was in high school. I even committed them to memory. They have remained in my memory all of these years, but the meaning of the verses has changed as I have grown older.

When I was in high school, I equated discipline mainly with punishment. Consequently, when the writer says earlier, in verse seven of this passage, to endure hardship as discipline, I had an idea in the back of my mind that difficulties in my life were punishment for not being as good as I should be.

I believed difficulties were just me getting what I deserved. God was punishing me so I would stop doing certain things. Oftentimes I wasn't even sure what those things were. I just knew I wasn't living up to God's standards, so He needed to discipline me, to punish me.

This is one of the common misconceptions many people have about Christianity. They think of God as someone who sits in heaven waiting to punish us when we're not good. This idea is so pervasive in the world that it is hard for us not to unwittingly take on this same misconception.

Today, though, when I looked a little deeper into this passage, I noticed the original word translated as discipline is not punishment, but rather training or educating. So, when it says God disciplines us, it is saying God is teaching or training us. It is spiritual education.

The especially wonderful thing is God does not discipline us, or teach us, merely for the sake of learning. He has a much greater intention. The writer says God is disciplining us, or training us, to share in His holiness.

As God disciplines us, we learn to lean into God's holiness while we face our hardships. We keep moving forward through difficulties trusting God is cultivating our minds and our hearts, conforming us to His holiness. He is making us spiritually mature.

When we are trained by God's discipline, the writer tells us it will produce a harvest of righteousness and peace. And this is what we all want, but we will miss out on it if we mistake God for a mean authoritarian who is looking to punish us, and torment us with unrealistic expectations.

Instead, true spiritual discipline trains us to share in God's holiness; to be mature enough to enjoy His relationship and trust in His goodness. It will turn us into people who can rest in the peace of Christ.

76
Re-Reading the Bible

Good morning kids! I am enjoying the experience of reading passages in the Bible I have read over and over throughout the past forty years, and seeing them in completely new ways. I feel like God has been blessing me with some new wisdom, which I am so grateful for.

This made me think of Solomon, though, who was blessed with vast wisdom, but he was not faithful. His wisdom was intellectual, but it was not lived out in his life. I want to both seek wisdom and become more faithful in my pursuit of Jesus.

It says in James 1:23-25:

"For if you listen to the word and don't obey, it is like glancing at your face in a mirror. You see yourself, walk away, and forget what you look like. But if you look carefully into the perfect law that sets you free, and if you do what it says and don't forget what you heard, then God will bless you for doing it."

I want to read scripture, to look carefully into God's perfect law, and continue to learn, to grow deeper in wisdom. But I also want to be protected from the arrogance that assumes just because I've read certain passages several times, I have learned all there is to know.

This would be like never running a trail twice, assuming since I ran it once, I saw all there was to see on that trail.

In reality, I run so many trails over and over. There are even certain special trails I prioritize. I make sure to run them at least once or twice every year, because I know I will experience them a little differently each time.

Consequently, over the years I have gathered many pictures taken from the exact same places. But one may be at midday on a clear blue summer day, while another may be at sunset. Or maybe the clouds on the horizon are dramatic. Or maybe it is autumn and the leaves are at their peak color. And other times it might be during a gentle snowstorm. The pictures are from the same spot, but it is not the same experience every time.

When I show up and keep myself open to what I might see; when I don't assume the view will be the same every time I go to these places; the landscape continues to reveal great and beautiful things I hadn't seen before.

I think it is the same with the Bible.

We need to guard against being so arrogant as to assume there is no benefit in studying passages we have studied before, because as we develop in our faith and maturity, we will be transforming, so our perspectives of certain passages in the Bible will often transform as well. When we follow Jesus, we will be changing people, so certain things will resonate with us differently at different ages, because we become, in some ways, actually different people.

And wouldn't it be sad if the Bible impacted us the same at 45 as it had at 35, or 25, or 15. That would not be the Bible's fault. It would be a sign we aren't growing. It would mean we had sealed ourselves off from the transforming power of God's grace and love.

The Bible is like a mirror that reveals who we are at any given time. As we change, we will see it differently, just as, when we look in the mirror, we will look a little different from one year to the next.

77
His Name is Near

Good morning kids! This morning I opened up Psalm 75, and I didn't make it past the first verse. The writer opens this psalm by saying:

"We give thanks to you, O God, we give thanks because your Name is near."

I was struck by how it says God's Name is near rather than simply saying God is near. I think it is because the essence, or the unique character of a person, is somehow hidden in their name.

When I start my day in the silent house each morning, I always begin in prayer. It is very simple. I think of God and try to make myself present to Him. And then I often say each of your names one at a time – M... K... S.

When I say your names, different images come before me that are specific to each of you. As I make my way through your names, one at a time, it is as if each of you are nearby in the wonder of your specific gifts and personalities.

I am not always sure what to pray for, so I often just think your name, and this somehow makes you present so I can offer each of you to God, trusting He can meet you where you are.

When I think of your names, I feel fondness for each of you

differently, because you are all so beautifully and wonderfully made. I feel gratitude for being able to share in each of your amazing journeys. I think this is what the psalmist means when he says God's Name is near.

As we get to know God, He reveals His unique character to each of us so we can know Him. As this relationship grows, so does the content of what comes to our minds when we meditate on His Name. We give thanks because we recognize more and more of the goodness and power hidden in His Name.

We may not always know what to say to God, but His Name is always near, so we really only need to say, "God; Lord; Jesus; Holy Spirit; thank you." And that is enough.

78
The Pharisee and the Tax Collector

Good morning kids! I've been thinking about Jesus' parable in Luke 18:9-14. I'm going to quote the full parable so you can see the full context:

> "To some who were confident of their own righteousness and looked down on everyone else, Jesus told this parable: "Two men went up to the temple to pray, one a Pharisee and the other a tax collector. The Pharisee stood by himself and prayed: 'God, I thank you that I am not like other people—robbers, evildoers, adulterers—or even like this tax collector. I fast twice a week and give a tenth of all I get.'
>
> "But the tax collector stood at a distance. He would not even look up to heaven, but beat his breast and said, 'God, have mercy on me, a sinner.'
>
> "I tell you that this man, rather than the other, went home justified before God. For all those who exalt themselves will be humbled, and those who humble themselves will be exalted."

Initially, this parable came to mind because I felt like Jesus could have been speaking directly to the Evangelical churches in the modern-day United States. Too often the church has departed from what I think God really intended the Church to be.

So many people work to be like the Pharisee, to present themselves as acceptable according to what they perceive the church's values to be. I'm afraid the objective of many churchgoers is to become "confident of their righteousness," as Luke said.

They are not looking at Jesus. They are looking at themselves. They think they have found the way to finally improve themselves; to become exceptional people.

This attitude marginalizes people like the tax collector, who went to the temple to find the God of mercy with a sense of desperation. Even if the church has become a little more "nice," seeming to welcome these people with words, there is all too often an uneasy judgmental undercurrent pulling beneath the surface.

Rather than leading these people to Jesus, the message often gets twisted. The church tends to step in and tell these people what they think they need to do to become justified; what they think they need to look like in order to accept Jesus. And then they go on to explain what these people will look like after they accept Him. They even quote the Bible a lot to prove they're right.

Their ideas of what they will look like are sadly generic.

For too many of us, the church's ideas of what we should look like will only further isolate the marginalized among us. This vision lacks the imagination to be open to what God really has in mind for us, with all of our uniqueness and beauty.

But Jesus says the tax collector is the one who is justified before God, because he recognized his own brokenness. He humbled himself before God because he realized, in the end, his only hope for redemption was the grace of God.

The Church is meant to be a place where we all come together to humble ourselves before the God of infinite grace and mercy and perfect love. This is not a one-time thing, where we humble ourselves before God once, and then expect ourselves to be exalted forever after.

Humbling ourselves before God is meant to become a permanent attitude of our hearts.

It is not because we are terrified of Him, but because we experience His mercy and come to know His love in a way only we can experience it. No one else gets to define how His love will change us. That is ultimately meant to be shared as a sacred and secret gift between Jesus and us alone.

79
I Am the Pharisee

Good morning kids! In the last text, I wrote about Jesus' parable of the Pharisee and the tax collector praying at the temple, and how the attitude of the Pharisee reminded me of some of the issues with the church today.

I think the things I said were true, but I realized I didn't tell the whole story, because more often than not, I am the Pharisee.

Jesus says in Luke 18:11-12:

"The Pharisee stood by himself and prayed: 'I thank you that I am not like other people—robbers, evildoers, adulterers— or even like this tax collector. I fast twice a week and give a tenth of all I get.'"

This translation says the Pharisee stood by himself and prayed. Some other translations go further and say he prayed with himself, or he prayed towards himself. Although he addressed his prayer to God, he was really praying to himself, about himself.

I have always struggled with prayer. I feel like I have a similar tendency to pray about myself in a sort of monologue. I am not necessarily always praising myself as the Pharisee does, but I am definitely talking more to myself than I am to God.

The Pharisee says he is thankful that he is not like these other sinful people, just as it is so easy for me to think similar thoughts. I can easily see other people plainly struggling in their lives, and I am relieved, or even glad, that at least I am not struggling as much as those other people.

I am not moved with love for those people. I rarely even offer up a weak intercessory prayer that God would meet those people in their brokenness.

The obvious truth is I have failed at most of the things I have been seriously tempted by all throughout my life. I might not have been tempted to be a thief or an adulterer, but when I was tempted to be proud... Well – I went all in.

Conveniently, for the upstanding among us, pride is not so easy to see. We can hide it easily. And if we realize it, and decide to confess it? ... People are comfortable with having compassion on us because it seems sort of safe. How bad is it anyway, they think? Having a little extra pride is practically an American value.

The Pharisee is not only proud. As he prays to himself, he goes on to admonish himself for fasting twice a week and tithing faithfully. The implication is, God is indebted to him. His view of God is transactional, not personal.

But the tax collector went home justified. He was able to look inside himself and recognize the reality of his plight. He was completely aware of his shortcomings, and it filled him with sorrow. So, he knelt before God, not even confident enough to look upwards. And God recognized him. He met him in his brokenness.

I am tired of praying to myself; of performing for God, and setting my expectations before Him regarding how He can answer my prayers and meet my needs. I am feeling my brokenness in a raw and painful way this year.

I think it's an answer to prayer. It's not the answer I wanted, but it is the answer I needed, so I can become more like the tax collector, so I can kneel face-down before God and honestly plead for His mercy and loving kindness.

80
Being Present in our Sorrow

Good morning kids! I have one last thought about the parable of the Pharisee and the tax collector. I want to look at only the tax collector today. Luke says in 18:13:

"But the tax collector stood at a distance. He would not even look up heaven, but beat his breast and said, 'God, have mercy on me, a sinner.'"

This man was full of grief and sorrow. I suspect this was not the first time he had experienced grief and sorrow over what had become of his life.

Presumably, earlier in his life, he most likely did what most of us do when we are confronted with grief and sorrow over the choices we have made. He probably worked harder. Or had a drink. Or went on a vacation. Or went to a party. He probably did whatever he could to avoid his grief and sorrow; to put it out of his mind; to keep it buried where he would not have to look at it.

But this time, he went to the temple to pray. He experienced his grief. He did not avoid it. He knelt in his sorrow before God.

It says in Ecclesiastes 7:3:

"Sorrow is better than laughter, because a sad face is good for the heart."

It is obviously not a bad thing to enjoy a vacation or a party. As it says earlier in Ecclesiastes, there are times to laugh and dance. Yet, sorrow is better than laughter because we are transformed by our grief and sorrow. Being present in grief and sorrow prepares our hearts to fully experience joy.

The tax collector was experiencing deep grief and sorrow over the realization of a life wasted, but not all griefs and sorrows are so large. We experience a tinge of grief and sorrow almost every day, even in the smallest things, because we recognize again and again that we are sinful people in need of His mercy.

God has allowed us to have these kinds of negative emotions intentionally. They are intended to get our attention.

God is calling out to us in these things, and if we are paying attention, they should be calling us to grief and sorrow. God wants us to be aware of the effects of our poor decisions and attitudes, so we don't continue to live as slaves to these things.

He wants us to recognize them, and to be sad, because a sad face is good for the heart.

Like with the tax collector, our grief and sorrow, for large things and small things, will open up a space for the God of mercy to lead us into the freedom and joy we all long for.

81
He Will Never Leave Us nor Forsake Us

Good morning kids! The Bible is a big and sometimes confusing book. And God is massive and beyond comprehension in many ways. But at the heart of it all, we only need to remember that God came to us in the shape of a person – Jesus Christ.

I keep thinking of God's promise first spoken in Deuteronomy 31:6. Moses was passing the leadership of the Israelites onto Joshua, who would be the one to take them out of the desert and into the promised land. He was told God would be with them, that "He (would) never leave you nor forsake you."

This promise of God was repeated again four hundred years later by David, and then again three hundred years later by Isaiah, and then a hundred years later by Jeremiah. God's promise, "never will I leave you nor forsake you," rings down throughout history.

And then, one day, this promise was made flesh when Jesus was born into human history.

Jesus, the promise of God, will never leave us nor forsake us. His faithfulness has no contingencies. It does not require us to behave in a particular way to earn His favor. He is simply there. Always.

I believe He was saying He will never leave us nor forsake us, even if we are not seeking for Him.

Moreover, He will be the One who seeks for us instead. He will believe in us. He will leave the 99 to seek for the one who is lost.

When he says he will not leave us nor forsake us, He was not only talking to Christians.

He came for the salvation of the entire world, regardless of their backgrounds or their nationalities or their personal stories. I believe He is saying He will never leave us nor forsake us regardless of who we are. I believe He came to save every last one of us.

Made in the USA
Monee, IL
22 February 2023

28460282R00105